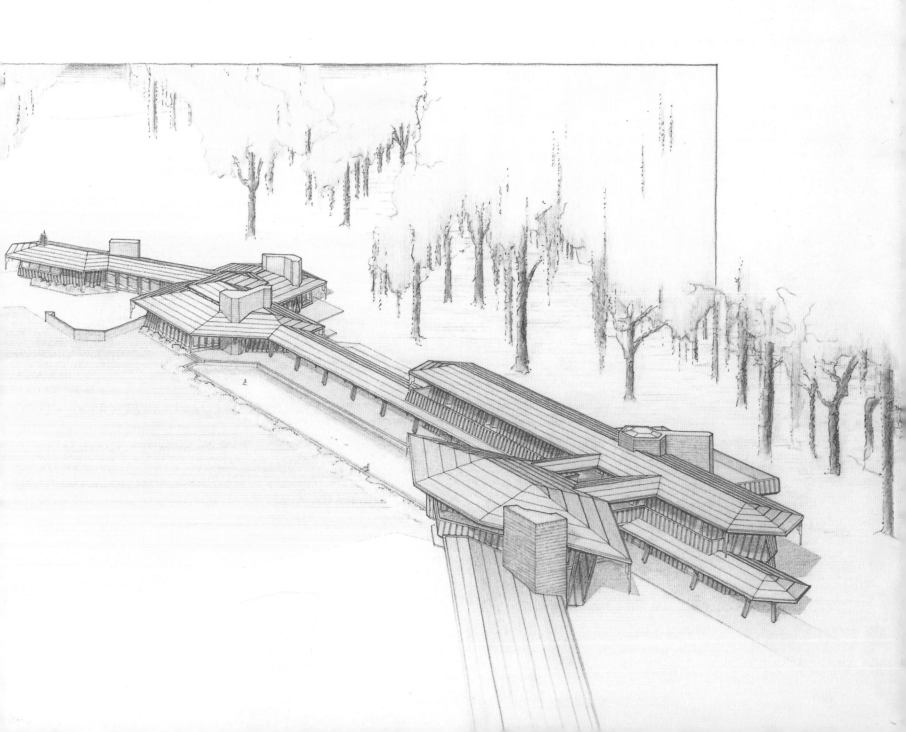

AULDBRASS

FRANK LLOYD WRIGHT'S SOUTHERN PLANTATION

AULDBRASS

FRANK LLOYD WRIGHT'S SOUTHERN PLANTATION

Second Edition

DAVID G. DE LONG

RIZZOLI
NEW YORK

Paris London Milan

NOTE: Images of photographs and drawings from the Frank Lloyd Wright Archives are identified by the abbreviation, FLWA. The Frank Lloyd Wright drawings are copyright © 2003, 2010 The Frank Lloyd Wright Foundation, Scottsdale, AZ. New photographs by Anthony Peres, Paul Rocheleau, Alan Weintraub, and David Soliday are individually identified.

COVER
MAIN HOUSE
Auldbrass, with kitchen at left and pergola at right. Anthony Peres, 2010

ENDPAPERS
AULDBRASS RENDERING
Eric Lloyd Wright

Second Edition

Published in the United States of America in 2011
by
RIZZOLI INTERNATIONAL PUBLICATIONS, INC.
300 Park Avenue South, New York, NY 10010
www.rizzoliusa.com

ISBN: 978-0-8478-3616-1

Library of Congress Control Number: 2010934530

Original edition first published in 2003, hardboud with jacket, ISBN: 978-0-8478-2536-3; LCCN: 2002115823

© 2011 Rizzoli International Publications, Inc.
Text © 2011 David G. De Long
"A Wright Angle" © 2011 Joel Silver
Photography © 2011 (photography copyrights held for individual photographs by each photographer, respectively, as identified in caption)

Photography for Epilogue was taken especially for second edition by Anthony Peres.

Designed by Abigail Sturges

Printed and bound in China

2011 2012 2013 2014 2015 /
10 9 8 7 6 5 4 3 2 1

 **CONTENTS**

INTRODUCTION

During his long and prolific career, Frank Lloyd Wright designed more than 1,000 buildings, but only one southern plantation: Auldbrass. Yet in that single commission he reconfigured an entire building type, seeking, as did his client, to revitalize a lost lifestyle. For Auldbrass not only reflects Wright's response to specific circumstance, but also his pursuit of archetypes, of solutions that achieved universality through redefined meanings of use and through celebration of place. The result was like no other plantation ever seen.

The commission proved long and difficult. It began in 1938 when C. Leigh Stevens, who would prove to be one of Wright's more demanding clients, challenged Wright to conceive a new kind of plantation, one that would address issues of contemporary use and economics while remaining strongly evocative of its southern location. Construction began in the fall of 1940, after a prolonged period of design. Yet the outbreak of World War II soon brought work to a stop. When construction resumed, problems of material shortages that had bedeviled the project before the war continued for several years after.

Wright's unusual design proved resistant to familiar conventions of building, confounding local builders and adding immeasurably to costs. Stevens remained supportive of Wright's vision, yet suffered from financial upheaval in his business and from personal upheavals as well. Work no sooner seemed under control than Stevens asked for more changes or new additions, tasks that Wright willingly undertook until his death in 1959. Stevens died three years later, leaving Auldbrass unfinished, a tantalizing record of Wright's genius and Stevens's perseverance.

In the years that followed, Stevens's daughter, Jessica Stevens Loring, and her husband, Stanton D. Loring, maintained the large, still incomplete estate with dedication. Subsequent owners, however, abandoned its care, and it fell gradually into a ruinous state. Its fortunes were reversed by a new owner, Joel Silver, who has invested heavily and with his own dedication not only to rescue it from decay, but also to complete it as Wright had envisioned, and as Stevens had wished. It stands at last as the archetypal image Wright conceived, central to a full understanding of his brilliant career. And it works in a manner Stevens could no doubt have accepted, had he lived to enjoy the elegance of rural leisures it now provides. What follows is the story of Auldbrass—of its original client, of its site, of its initial design and construction, of the changing vicissitudes of its fortunes, and of its restoration and continuing development.

Edgar Kaufmann, jr., the celebrated Wright scholar, first brought Auldbrass to my attention and urged me to undertake this study. Kaufmann had apprenticed with Wright in the early 1930s and shepherded his father through the construction of Fallingwater, one of Wright's most famous designs.[1] Over the years that followed, while associated with the Museum of Modern Art and later as an adjunct professor at Columbia University, Kaufmann continued his studies of Wright's work. Wright came to respect Kaufmann's judgment, as their collaboration on several publications indicates,[2] and Kaufmann considered Auldbrass one of Wright's most important designs. His views were seconded by another Wright scholar, Henry-Russell Hitchcock, who, at Wright's invitation, wrote the first scholarly account of Wright's work, published in 1942 as *In the Nature of Materials*.[3]

In the spring of 1987, Kaufmann invited me to accompany him on a visit to Auldbrass so that I might begin my work with first-hand knowledge. We were the guests of Victoria Newhouse, then head of the Architectural History Foundation, who had organized the trip. We arrived in Savannah aboard a chartered jet and transferred to a waiting limousine that would take us to Yemassee, South Carolina, about an hour away. The drive proved no less special than the flight, for Joel Silver, the new owner of Auldbrass, had arranged for a police escort. After such welcoming extravagances, Auldbrass itself proved a startling contrast. Seemingly abandoned, with various buildings obscured by undergrowth, it indeed lay in a ruinous state. A worker who had performed odd jobs for the original owner showed us about, adding to the sense of desolation by recalling past days of splendor.

This state of decay and abandonment was about to change. Silver had retained Eric Lloyd Wright, Wright's grandson, to undertake a massive restoration of Auldbrass. Eric joined us on our visit and began to outline the vast campaign of rebuilding that would be undertaken to restore Auldbrass to the image of southern ease that Wright envisioned (fig. 11).

Among those enthralled by Wright's concept are four people with the sort of determination and vision essential to the realization of any great work of architecture: C. Leigh Stevens, the original client; Jessica Stevens Loring and her husband, Stanton D. Loring, his daughter and son-in-law; and Joel Silver, the present owner. They, too, have understood the importance of Auldbrass in the work of Frank Lloyd Wright.

I will remain forever indebted to Edgar Kaufmann, jr. who was, during his lifetime, (to borrow Wright's term for Louis Sullivan) my Lieber Meister. I am also deeply indebted to Victoria Newhouse, who has provided ongoing support and encouragement for this and many other projects, and who in particular has offered valued suggestions for this book.

PREVIOUS PAGES
FIG. 10
MAIN HOUSE FROM LAKE
Auldbrass, looking across the lake in early evening. Paul Rocheleau, 2003

To Joel Silver I owe much, for in addition to allowing me unrestricted access to Auldbrass and its remarkable archive, he has met with me there and in Los Angeles to discuss the manuscript of this book and to share his insights. He has also generously provided new color photography as well as other record photographs, and he has remained steadfast in seeing that I complete this project. I also offer my thanks to his wife, Karyn; to his associate, Pam Martin; to his manager at Auldbrass, Scott McNair; to the assistant manager, Margaret Martin; and to the many others at Auldbrass and at Silver Pictures who have so kindly assisted.

Early on in this project I met on several occasions—in Charleston, at Auldbrass, and in their home—with Jessica Stevens Loring and her husband, Stanton Loring. They were not only gracious hosts on these occasions, but also shared their knowledge of Auldbrass and their extensive family archive of documents and photographs relating to its design and construction, and they carefully reviewed and offered valued suggestions for the manuscript of this book. I thank them for their kind help.

My thanks also to Eric Lloyd Wright, who expressed his perceptive understanding of Auldbrass during meetings there and at his Malibu studio, and who, with Joel Silver's support, created the new perspective in his grandfather's style to show a completed final image of the plantation. And I am grateful to Donna Butler and Thomas Schmidt, both of whom were involved with Auldbrass during a critical period of its history, for providing valued information and for reviewing portions of the manuscript.

Full research on Auldbrass would not have been possible, nor Wright's original drawings and letters made accessible

and (for the drawings) readied for publication, without the extraordinary help I have received over the years from the Frank Lloyd Wright Archives at Taliesin West. For this help and for sharing their special knowledge, I give my thanks to Bruce Brooks Pfeiffer, Director of the Frank Lloyd Wright Archives, and to his hard-working colleagues at Taliesin West, including Oscar Muñoz, Margo Stipe, Indira Berndtson, and Penny Fowler. Among others who helped in archival matters, I thank Julia Moore Converse, Director, and William Whitaker, Collections Manager, of the Architectural Archives at the University of Pennsylvania. At the Library of Congress, my special thanks to C. Ford Peatross, Curator of Prints and Photographs; at the Canadian Centre for Architecture, Phyllis Lambert, Founder and now Chairman of the Board, Nicholas Olsberg, now Director, and Helen Malkin, Chief of Exhibitions; at the Avery Art and Architectural Library at Columbia, Janet Parks, Curator of Drawings; at the Vitra Design Museum, Alexander von Vegesack, Director, and Mathias Schwsartz-Clauss, his assistant; at Exhibitions International, David Hanks and Joan Rosasco.

Much of my research on Auldbrass was made possible by grants which I received and by facilities which in some cases came with those grants. My thanks, then, to the Getty Center for the History of Art and Humanities, to the University of Pennsylvania, to the John Simon Guggenheim Memorial Foundation, and to the American Academy in Rome. It was as a Visiting Scholar at the Getty that I began focused research on Auldbrass, with the sponsorship of a Research Grant from the University of Pennsylania that I made my first extended visits to Auldbrass, and while a Guggenheim Fellow at the American Academy in Rome, where I was also the first James Marston Fitch Resident in Historic Preservation, that I found the ideal location as well as time (during work on another project) to actually organize my research and begin writing.

I would like to thank many colleagues who have offered welcome suggestions related to this project, including Anthony Alofsin, H. Allen Brooks, Daniel Castor, Adele Chatfield-Taylor, Thomas Hine, Neil Levine, Frank Matero, R. Craig Miller, Witold Rybczynski, Kathryn Smith, Anne Whiston Spirn, Robert Sweeney, Jack Quinan, and Lynda Waggoner. Among administrative assistants at the University of Pennsylvania, my thanks to Jean Wolf and Suzanne Hyndman; among my student assistants, Seth Hinshaw and, especially Stacey Donahoe. For special photography, I am grateful to Will Brown, Anthony Peres, and David Soliday; for the computer renderings, Robert Lesnick, Rob Henson, and Tom Crews. Finally, my very special thanks to my editor at Rizzoli, David Morton; the assistant editor, Douglas Curran; and to the designer of this book, Abigail Sturges.

FIG. 11
MAIN HOUSE
Auldbrass, spring 1987. Left to right: Victoria Newhouse, Edgar Kaufmann, jr., Eric Lloyd Wright. Author

A WRIGHT ANGLE

When I first learned of Auldbrass Plantation and it was clear that I might be able to acquire it, I was struck by an ironic fact. 1939, the year Auldbrass was designed, was the year that Margaret Mitchell's legendary *Gone With The Wind* was finally brought to the screen. That meant that just as audiences across the nation saw that first shot of Tara, the quintessential antebellum Southern plantation, Frank Lloyd Wright was conceiving Auldbrass. America had a memorable image of a grand drive past a stately allée of live oak trees to a crisp white columned neoclassical building. Auldbrass could not be more of an antithesis.

People never know what to expect when they pass through the streamlined geometric gates of Wright's version of a Southern plantation. The simple red gravel drive through a grove of live oaks to an elegant cluster of warm toned cypress buildings always boggles their minds.

When I first made that drive in the fall of 1986, I certainly didn't know what to expect. I knew from the pictures of the complex in Futagawa's monograph[1] that the place was dilapidated, but I had just been through the restoration of one of Wright's textile-block houses in California, so I was ready for a new adventure.

One could easily see the genius of Wright's concept of a gentleman's farm in rural South Carolina. The original owner, Leigh Stevens, had wanted a retreat from his hectic life. Unfortunately, the complete plan was never fully realized.

Blinded by my enthusiasm and excitement for a new project, I saw Auldbrass as a script ready to be produced. Twenty interconnecting buildings designed by Frank Lloyd Wright in a pastoral setting that I could get for a good deal. How could I go wrong?

I must have been out of my mind.

When discussing his cherished Japanese wood-block prints, Wright used to say, "They always find the ones they love." I can't help but think that Auldbrass chose me as much as I chose it. When I first started this journey I had made only a few movies, I had no family and I didn't have a clue where I would get the money to accomplish the Herculean task ahead. I just believed I would do it.

When you make a movie you never know how it's going to turn out. Everyone has the best intentions. You start with the best script you can get, the best director, the best actors, the best music, the best everything. You always hope it will work. Sometimes it does, many times it doesn't. You never know.

Somehow with Auldbrass I knew. Frank Lloyd Wright had provided the script; he was the director, the actors, and the music. I've always felt that there was a great similarity between the design and construction of a building and the production of a movie. Both start in the exact same fashion, a bunch of ideas on a piece of paper. Through a very complex process of creativity, negotiation, and compromise something is brought to life that could last forever. With Auldbrass I felt as long as I followed Wright's plan it would be a hit.

My life is different now. Since acquiring Auldbrass I have married and made many more movies, including *Predator*, a couple of *Die Hards*, four *Lethal Weapons* and *The Matrix* trilogy. Now, with my wife and our adorable son, Auldbrass has become a much-needed constant in our hectic lives. We celebrate every Thanksgiving and Christmas there surrounded by family and friends. As I watch my son, his cousins and their friends grow up, I see how Auldbrass delights them as it does everyone who drives through its gates.

At the same time, however, Auldbrass is constantly changing. There is always something to upgrade, something new to build, something else to plan and accomplish. Auldbrass is a great unfinished story. It is it's own sequel. There are always new characters being introduced, new plot twists, new set-ups and of course, new pay-offs.

Maybe I never want to finish Auldbrass. It makes me work hard so that I can keep it alive. Every time I arrive there I am again awestruck. It is a magical place. Like a movie, it makes one believe that anything is possible.

Tara is frozen in celluloid. In all its Technicolor glory, it looks today exactly as it did in 1939. In sixty-five years it hasn't changed. But Auldbrass continues to evolve. It continues to find new uses for itself while providing me new creative challenges. I am only a custodian of this testament to Frank Lloyd Wright's genius. As such, I feel it is my responsibility to maintain its beauty and integrity and try to make it my best production ever.

— Joel Silver

Brentwood, California
August 2003

CHAPTER 1

LEIGH STEVENS AND THE BEGINNINGS OF AULDBRASS

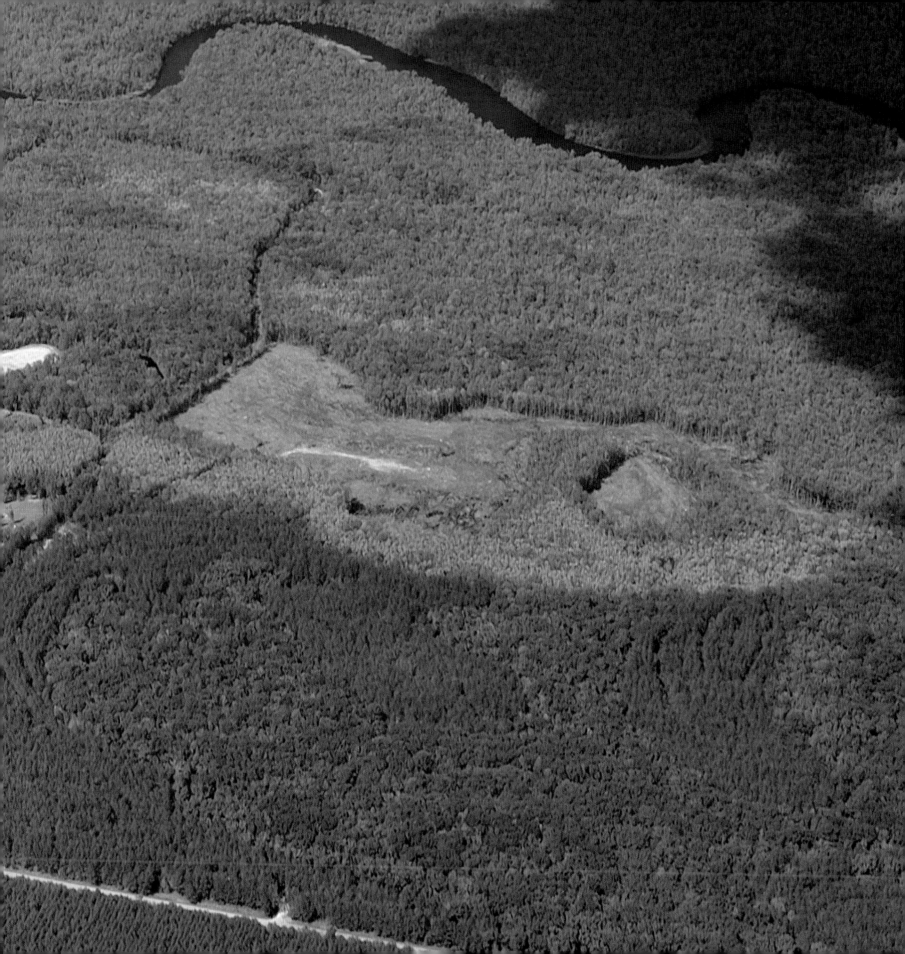

Nearing the height of his newly revived career in the late 1930s, Frank Lloyd Wright conceived new forms for the idealized society he had begun to envision. Auldbrass embodies this quest. Yet its initial realization depended largely on a remarkable client: Charles Leigh Stevens (1895–1962). Together with other clients of Wright's later career—clients that included, in particular, Edgar Kaufmann, sr., H. C. Johnson, and Harold C. Price—Stevens provided commissions that led to some of Wright's most extraordinary achievements.[1] These clients were similar in their creative manipulation of business and industry, perhaps partly accounting for their interest in Wright. Like Stevens, their fortunes were largely self-made, they challenged conventional ways of operation, and they seemed to welcome in Wright a reciprocating force of their own genius.

Stevens's relationship to the world of business, however, was more complicated, and more obscure, than was typical of Wright's other clients. Described as one of the world's leading industrial consultants, Stevens advised countless firms and several governments on how to improve productivity. Yet his advice was often given in confidence, and left largely unrecorded, so that his specific achievements, while renowned at the time, remain elusive.

Stevens was born in Muskegon, Michigan, on May 24, 1895, and given the names of two of his father's closest friends: J. Charles Ireland and Leigh B. Smith.[2] They acknowledged this "honor recently conferred" in a letter written shortly after Stevens's birth.[3]

Stevens's father, Clifton Delmar Stevens, owned and operated the Muskegon Boiler Works, which had been established in 1865 and which he had purchased around 1890. Its principal activity was the fabrication of steel—as plate, as boilers, as giant exhaust stacks, and the like. Stevens recalled that his father had ". . . worked me in it just about the time I was able to walk, so that my early background was primarily steel and steel fabrication."[4] The company, later called MBW, Inc., has remained in the Stevens family for over a century, most recently under the direction of Stevens's nephew, Charles Leigh Stevens II.[5] The family took pride in their enterprise, and also in the earlier work of Stevens's maternal grandfather, Charles Byron Field, a merchant described as "the river boss of the Muskegon River" who drove a billion feet of timber down the river to the mill.[6]

Around the time of Stevens's birth, his father built a substantial house in Muskegon, and it was there that Stevens spent his childhood years. An early photograph shows him beside the house, holding the family's horse; near the front of the driveway, his older sister, Helen, stands protectively beside their infant brother, Paul, comfortably seated in his stroller (fig. 17).[7] The house was apparently well-staffed by servants, and life must have been comfortable; Stevens later recalled a summer when he briefly substituted for the family's chauffeur.[8]

Stevens graduated from the Muskegon High School in the spring of 1912, and that same year completed his studies of mechanical drawing, woodworking, and metal casting at the Hackley Manual Training School.[9] To broaden his knowledge of industrial production, he entered the Sibley College of Mechanical Engineering at Cornell University in the fall. There he took one of the country's first courses in industrial engineering, taught by Professor Dexter Kimball, later Dean of the College of Engineering. Yet Stevens failed to graduate. He left Cornell in 1916, deficient in Latin and with unfulfilled requirements in Physics. He later petitioned for his degree; the university offered to substitute French or some other foreign language for the Latin requirement, and signaled willingness to negotiate "a little adjustment" for the "matter of the Physics,"[10] but by then Stevens's career was sufficiently advanced that any interruption would have been a bother, and apparently no further action was taken.

Shortly after leaving Cornell he began working for his father in the Muskegon Boiler Works, and late that summer, on September 16, 1916, married Jessica Agnes Thompson of Madison, Wisconsin. During the next few years he gradually worked his way up in the company, reaching the position of Assistant Superintendent and supervising some 30 to 40 employees. Inspired by Professor Kimball's course at Cornell, he also implemented an incentive sys-

tem—new at the time—that offered a 40 percent bonus to those workers who met high standards of production.[11] Already he was beginning to organize the energy of those with whom he worked.

A son, named Clifton Delmar Stevens II after Stevens's father, was born on May 10, 1918, and a daughter, Jessica Ann Stevens, on May 16, 1920.[12] By then he had moved ambitiously to another position, lured away by one of his father's consultants, Charles Eugene Bedaux (1886–1944). Born in France, Bedaux had come to the United States in 1906, and by 1919, when he was associated with Stevens's father, had established himself as an efficiency expert of considerable skill.[13] While advising the owner of the Muskegon Boiler Works he met the owner's son, and was sufficiently impressed to offer young Stevens a position in his own office. Bedaux would continue to prosper, at least until World War II, when he was accused of illegal business arrangements with Germany. Before then, he had bought and restored a fifteenth-century estate in the Loire Valley—the Chateau de Candé—where his guests, the Duke and Duchess of Windsor, were married with widespread publicity in 1937,[14] barely a year before Stevens would embark on the creation of his own estate.

However Bedaux's increasing prominence may have affected Stevens, he profited more immediately from his position in Bedaux's firm, later crediting Bedaux with teaching him the basic principles of production management and by 1924 ammassing sufficient capital to buy the New England branch of Bedaux's business for $100,000.[15] Thus at age 29 he found himself the sole owner of the C. L. Stevens Company, an industrial consulting firm employing some six engineers that he hired from Bedaux's firm. He claimed he made his first million dollars that same year,[16] having already attained "national distinction in the field of time and motion studies, and in other means of expanding production."[17] He continued to run his company until his death in 1962, employing upwards of 25 engineers.[18] The ambition that led to such early success, and a seemingly relentless determination to manage complicated operations, especially when none before him had succeeded, served Stevens well in the building of Auldbrass. Of these qualities there is scattered evidence, but ultimately it becomes clear. Describing Stevens's accomplishments in 1953, Donald K. David, then Dean of the Harvard Graduate School of Business Administration, wrote,

> I first knew Mr. Stevens in 1931 when I became President of the American-Maize-Products Company and retained him to help us with a difficult production problem in an out-of-date plant. He was so successful and his advice so conservative and sound that I kept him as a consultant for the remaining years I was President of that firm, or until 1942. With his help we succeeded in modernizing the

FIG. 17
STEVENS FAMILY HOUSE
207 5th Street, Muskegon, Mich. 1902.
Courtesy Jessica Stevens Loring

C. LEIGH STEVENS HOUSE

Westwood, Mass. ca. 1927. Paul J. Weber, photographer; courtesy Jessica Stevens Loring, and Perry Dean Rogers/Partners Architects.

plant and increasing its output by roughly 50%, and despite a 40% increase in hourly rates, ended up with a total labor payroll somewhat less than where we started.[19]

Serving as consultant to hundreds of industries, Stevens himself described "great strides" in boosting production while keeping labor costs low; of his clients he claimed, "they have never lost a work load arbitration,"[20] advising management how to increase their returns while lowering production costs, whatever the field of industry being

addressed.[21] Always he defined even the largest and most impossible of projects in quantifiable terms so they could be effectively managed.

In professing loyalty to Charles Bedaux as his teacher, Stevens claimed he learned "that the work of men, their physical output, their potential ability to do work, is an absolute constant and that if it is an absolute constant then it is the only continuing denominator in industry."[22] This constant Stevens attempted to reduce to a mathematical formula that would govern the relationship between human energy and industrial production.[23] He came to develop what he called "Bedaux's principle," which he reduced to four often quoted points:

> 1. The ability of man in the mass to produce energy is an unchanging constant—individuals may vary in their ability, but man in the mass does not.
> 2. Industry basically is the application of man's energy to change the form or position of material with or without the assistance of machines.
> 3. By measuring the human energy required by any industrial process and at the same time measuring the effectiveness with which the energy is applied to that process a true universality of measurement is possible either momentarily or continually.
> 4. In other words, with 1, 2, and 3 above as postulates, it is possible to use various devices to measure the energy requirement of a given job and then get a standard value (in points) for that job—a value which is fixed and unchanging so long as there is no change in process.[24]

Perhaps the strongest constant of all was Stevens's belief in sustained, hard work:

> In my opinion, anyone who thinks that a man can't work more than 40 hours a week or 8 hours a day is just plain wrong. The inherent capacity of men to do work is tremendous. America, in my opinion, is beginning to lose an understanding of what the true capabilities of men are. One of the most potent factors in the world today is the fact that the Far East doesn't know anything about a 40-hour week. They work something more like an 84-hour week and they have just as much inherent ability to do good work as we ever had.[25]

Stevens did not restrict his energies to industrial production. He became active on various boards during the 1920s, for example the Reed-Prentice Co., of Worcester, Massachusetts, and the American Trust Company.[26] He also began to acquire real estate. By 1925, he had purchased 130 acres of farmland in what became the Boston suburb of Westwood. There he built a new home, designed by the Boston firm of Perry, Shaw, & Hepburn (fig. 18). He had chosen a prominent firm; in 1926, they were to be named restoration architects of Williamsburg.[27]

To supervise the construction of his new home, Stevens turned to a Muskegon friend: Olaf Otto, who would later oversee building operations at Auldbrass.[28] It was a relatively small building, described by his daughter as a copy of a French cottage and meant ultimately as the gardener's house for the extensive estate Stevens envisioned. Yet only the basement of the larger house was excavated before the stock market crash of 1929 ended Stevens's plans for fur-

ther development.[29] He lived in the "gardener's cottage" with his wife until they separated in 1934, and it remained in the possession of his descendants until 1993, when it was sold by the estate of his son.[30]

While the Great Depression put an end to Stevens's immediate plans for real estate development, it provided other opportunities for the acquisition of land, and these Stevens pursued aggressively, eventually acquiring the property where he would build Auldbrass. Among Stevens's clients in the 1930s was the Lee Higgenson & Company of Boston, and among properties this company controlled was the Savannah River Lumber Company, with holdings that included some 80,000 acres of timberland in Georgia and South Carolina. Lumber businesses did not flourish during the Great Depression, and in the late 1930s the Savannah River Lumber Company slid into bankruptcy. Stevens, as advisor to Lee Higgenson & Company, was consulted on the rescue of their Savannah subsidiary. As part of his solution, it was reorganized as the Savannah River Lumber Corporation and its headquarters moved to Delaware. In lieu of a fee, Stevens took 40 percent of common stock in the new company, and sometime later became its sole owner.[31] During the early phases of these manipulations, in additional payment for "certain engineering and other services to the corporation," he negotiated for a 4,000 acre tract of land in South Carolina "known as the Old Brass or Jackson Tract." This contractual agreement between Stevens and the Savannah River Lumber Corporation is dated December 20, 1938, and is so defined that the land would pass into Stevens's ownership whether the new Corporation survived or not.[32] With his ownership of the future site of Auldbrass thus assured, he began immediately to make plans.

The Low Country land that Stevens acquired lies midway between Charleston and Savannah, within the Lower Coastal Plain of South Carolina and about twenty miles inland from the Atlantic coast. It is bordered on the northwest by the Combahee River, part of the drainage basin of St. Helena Sound. This is no ordinary feature, for the Combahee, together with the Ashepoo and Edisto rivers further north, form what is described as the "largest estuary on the Southeastern coastline of the United States" (fig. 19).[33] Geologists characterize the area as unusually flat, with low elevations extending further inland than is typically the case.[34] The highest point on Stevens's land, in fact, is barely twenty feet above the Combahee River—there are no visible slopes of any appreciable sort, rather an overwhelming sense of vast, level terrain (fig. 15). With soils suitable for cultivation, it lies just above a nearby flood plain of the Combahee River, on which hardwoods predominate together with varieties of pine. Beneath the soil lies a "veneer of Cretaceous and Cenozoic sediments which, in

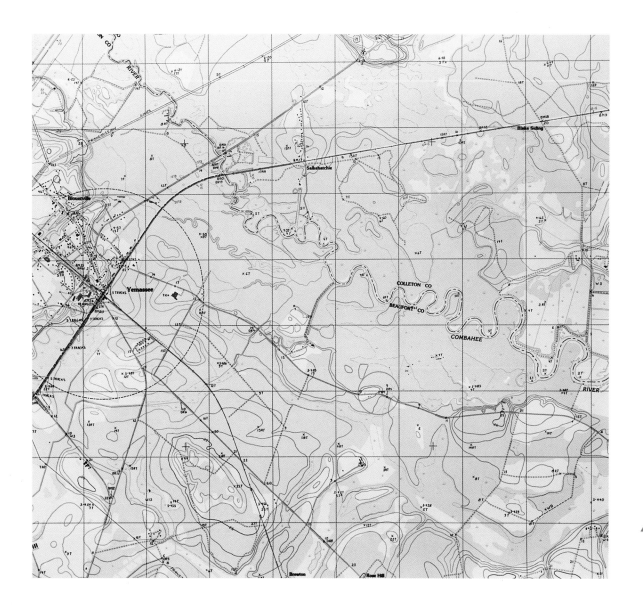

FIG. 19

YEMASSEE QUADRANGLE DETAIL

S.C., United States Geological Survey, 1988, with Auldbrass circled in red.

turn, overlie pre-Mesozoic crystalline rocks and tilted sedimentary rocks in buried Triassic-Jurassic basins."[35] At the surface lie outcroppings of Pleistocene sediments.[36]

When finally assembled, Stevens's property totaled 4,253 acres. The complicated history of overlapping ownerships and of various uses of these lands has been carefully documented by his daughter,[37] but can be summarized to suggest the layers of occupation that also lie beneath its surface.

During its early occupation, Indian trails led across the area to a ford on the Combahee River, and the roads and railroads that ultimately followed took this same course.[38] Colonization began in the 1670s, when planters from the West Indies were drawn to the area by a semi-tropical cli-

mate they judged superior to Barbados. Among the first to settle there were Edward and Arthur Middleton; their father, Captain Benjamin Middleton, was a noted planter on Barbados, and their descendants—one to become a signer of the Declaration of Independence—became prominent plantation owners.[39] In 1707, the area was designated by the General Assembly at Charles Town (later Charleston) as Yamasee [sic] Indian Land, but this was voided following the Indian uprising of 1715, in which several hundred people were killed and Charleston itself threatened. The area was next surveyed in 1731 and reallocated as a series of Crown Grants (fig. 20). Of the plantations that followed, five lay on Auldbrass land: Mount Pleasant, on which Auldbrass itself was built; to the west, Mount Alexander, Charlton, and Richfield; and to the east, Old Combahee.[40] Except for masonry ruins that survived into the twentieth century but have since been lost to view,[41] no buildings of this early period survive on Auldbrass land; but old bricks excavated during the construction of the main house at Auldbrass in 1940 indicate that it was built over the foundations of an earlier structure. This has been tentatively identified as the house of John Deas, which he had built before 1758, but no record of its design has been discovered.[42]

During the late eighteenth and early nineteenth centuries, South Carolina merchants profited greatly from Atlantic trade and converted portions of their earnings into landed estates. The vitality of this trade started to wane around 1820, and owners began to depend more fully on income derived from their land. The ownership of property became less casual and large plantations were developed. The profitability of these plantations depended increasingly on slaves, whose labor was essential in the cultivation of two principal cash crops: rice and sea island cotton. South Carolina has been described as "the greatest slave state of all," and large numbers were held by the owners of plantations that were, on the average, the largest estates in the country.[43] On these factors the economy of the area depended in the years before the Civil War.[44]

Certain Antebellum patterns bear on the later building of Auldbrass. Like Stevens, plantation owners in South Carolina tended to be absent for long periods, especially during summer months when they escaped the heat for cooler locations. It was necessary for workers to remain under the direction of responsible managers, a class below that of the privileged owners yet clearly above that of the workers themselves. This layered arrangement has been described as a special kind of "domestic servitude," and for it to work, owners had to establish an aura, or presence, that came to be symbolized by the visible status of the house itself. The fabled images of southern plantations reflect this definition of privileged identity.[45] Such houses could become obsessions, obscuring larger realities.

Early residents have written poignantly of the problem of leaving plantations untended for long periods, and of their power to distort workable reality in favor of family presence. William Elliott, a low-country planter who was educated at Harvard and also known as a sportsman, author, and legislator, wrote in 1846 of how, at the end of October, planters "entrenched in towns and villages, rushed forth to revisit their forsaken plantations. . . . The demons of pestilence, that for six months had rioted undisturbed in the dank vapors of our campagna . . . now . . . boomed off."[46] The importance of the Southern plantation

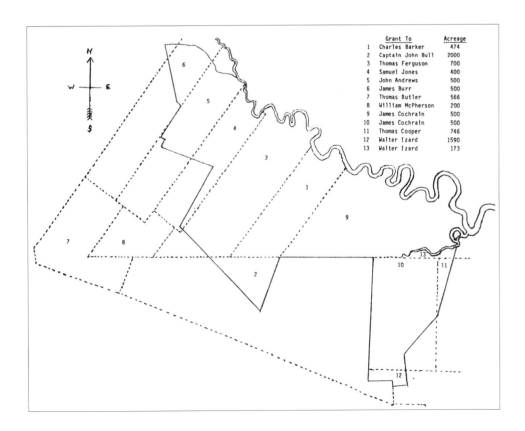

FIG. 20
**CROWN GRANTS
RELATING TO AULDBRASS**

From Jessica Stevens Loring, *Auldbrass, a Documented History Of Its South Carolina Lands*, Greenville, S.C.: Southern Historical Press, Inc., 1992, 8

	Grant To	Acreage
1	Charles Barker	474
2	Captain John Bull	2000
3	Thomas Ferguson	700
4	Samuel Jones	400
5	John Andrews	500
6	James Burr	500
7	Thomas Butler	566
8	William McPherson	200
9	James Cochrain	500
10	James Cochrain	500
11	Thomas Cooper	746
12	Walter Izard	1590
13	Walter Izard	173

house as symbol of both status and enduring family values is suggested by a statement of William Henry Trescot, who, following the Civil War, came back into possession of his plantation of 1,000 acres located in the Broad River, near Beaufort, a little more than twenty miles from Auldbrass.[47] Described as "a highly self-conscious and conscientious representative of his class and interests . . . ," he recalled,

> In many of our strongest convictions, in much of our most constant habits, we were an anachronism and an anomaly. . . . Ours was essentially a government of class and race.
>
> Great estates rather than great fortunes . . . were the ideals of Southern prosperity. . . . [The] tendency of Southern life was towards a home, not a house, not toward the exaggerated increase of individual wealth, but towards the creation and preservation of the family.[48]

One further aspect of pre-Civil War life near the future site of Auldbrass bears mention, for it figured in Stevens's plans and continues today to enhance the property: it was, and is, a hunter's paradise. This, too, had been emphasized early on by Elliott. He described his successful pursuits of wildcats, deer, and wild turkey, calling the area the "best hunting ground in Carolina," and chiding "city sportsmen" who hunted in Long Island and New Jersey, but got less in a week than Elliott claimed in a day. He continued, ". . .ye enthusiasts in sport, who import from our shores the game your own inhospitable winters deny to your wishes. . . ."[49]

The first mention of an Old Brass Plantation, or at least the first that can be documented, occurs in 1859, prior to the Civil War, in conjunction with the sale of the land to John H. Screven.[50] When he, in turn, sold the land in 1864 to William Middleton, a direct descendant of the Middletons who had settled in the area in the 1670s and who had become one of South Carolina's prominent families, it is again recorded as Old Brass.[51]

How the name Old Brass came to be connected with the land has been much researched, but facts remain elusive. In compiling the history of the lands of Auldbrass, Jessica Stevens Loring has determined that the name "Brass" was often recorded in plantation inventories to reflect the distinctive color of African American slaves who were also part Indian. The term "Old Brass" would indicate an older person of 60 years or more who was no longer required to work. One such person reportedly built a shack on that plantation's small landing on the Combahee River, at the end of the trail from inland fields, and there he remained, a kind of name-giving sentinel for what became known as Old Brass Landing. Far from being insignificant, such landings served for the receipt of supplies and shipment of crops to and from Charleston

before roads provided for such traffic, and the name held.[52] Others have claimed that the land was named by the owner of the plantation in honor of a slave named Old Brass who had saved the owner's daughter from drowning,[53] but for this there is no real evidence at all, and as Loring has made clear, "no owner lived on the plantation in the early 1800s and certainly would not have allowed a daughter to accompany him on his visits."[54]

Following the Civil War, the economy of the area underwent drastic change. Without slave labor, crops that had supported large plantations were no longer profitable, and many cultivated fields were abandoned. The stands of trees that began to grow—pine, sweet gum, and oak—provided another kind of cash crop, however, and timber interests began to stimulate renewed exploitation of the land. An ever growing interest in hunting also led to additional use.

During these post-Civil War years, patterns of ownership of the lands that would constitute Auldbrass plantation became more speculative in nature, again as recounted by Loring.[55] By 1900, much of the property had been assembled by James U. Jackson, a real estate developer in Augusta, Georgia, who created from it the Combahee Hunting Club. By 1919, after elaborate processes of transfers and sales among timber companies, it ended up being owned by the Savannah River Lumber Company, the very company that went bankrupt during the Depression and that was reorganized by Leigh Stevens as the Savannah River Lumber Corporation.

When Stevens came into ownership of the land in 1938, it lay within an area of fashionable winter retreat. The idea of having a southern plantation had taken root with wealthy northerners, particularly from the vicinity of New York, so that it became kind of "winter Newport."[56] Typically these northerners arrived with their horses in late October, at the beginning of the hunting season. The trip was relatively short—just under a day by train—and it brought them to a warmer, more salubrious climate. Had they chosen to go much further, everything would have been more complicated, especially the transport of horses, a feat comparatively simple if only one day or less were required. Having their own horses was essential to a full enjoyment of the hunt, and thus the geographic proximity of the area provided an added inducement for its development.

Most of the plantation houses these winter residents refurbished (or built anew) were given a traditional appearance, to judge by descriptions of social events. One exception was Mepkin Plantation, the winter home of Henry R. Luce, in Moncks Corner, South Carolina, about 100 miles distant from Auldbrass. Located on a 7,200-acre tract and completed in 1937 according to designs by

FIG. 21
EDWARD DURELL STONE,
MEPKIN PLANTATION
Moncks Corner, S.C., 1937, view toward
entrance. From Edward Durell Stone, *The Evolution
of an Architect*, New York: Horizon Press, 1962, 48

FOLLOWING PAGES
FIG. 22
THE LAKE
Auldbrass grounds. Paul Rocheleau, 1994

Edward Durell Stone (1902–1978), it had been conceived
as a modern interpretation of the southern plantation (fig.
21). Essentially an essay in restrained modernism, it dif-
fered greatly in character from what Wright would shortly
design.[57] Big Survey, Solomon Guggenheim's 1200-acre
plantation and hunting retreat, lay across the Combahee
River in Colleton County, and Stevens's daughter remembers the Guggenheims as guests at Auldbrass.[58] As such
prominent family names indicate, the land that Stevens had
acquired was hardly within a remote backwater. And the
area has continued to remain appealing; in 2001, its
"hauntingly beautiful landscape" was described as "one of
the largest swaths of undeveloped land on the Eastern
Seaboard" and a favorite locale for hunters.[59]

FRANK LLOYD WRIGHT AND THE DESIGN OF AULDBRASS

In 1938, when Leigh Stevens asked Frank Lloyd Wright to design Auldbrass, Wright was in his early seventies and a full generation older than Stevens, who was only forty-three. Yet retirement was as far from Wright's mind as it was from Stevens's, for both men were nearing the height of their careers, whatever their age differences.

By 1900, when he was in his early thirties, Wright had designed buildings that would change the course of architecture, buildings that were soon to be recognized as forming the basis of modern design. Thus he established himself as a leader in his field at an early age, as would Stevens. Yet only ten years later, just as his work was beginning to be widely acclaimed in Europe, Wright's career entered a period of decline. This was largely precipitated by his elopement with the wife of a client, leading to social ostracism and a drastic reduction in commissions.[1] But his own determination to change the direction of his work added to the problem, for new approaches he tried were more than ever at odds with the expectations of his day.

During the next two decades, from around 1910 to the early 1930s, Wright sustained himself through concentrated effort on a few commissions. Some were of major importance, such as the Imperial Hotel in Tokyo (1913–23), but insufficiently appreciated at the time. During these same decades, Wright suffered personal upheavals of epic proportion. Taliesin, his country home and studio, was twice destroyed by fire, the first time by arson, when members of his extended family were savagely murdered. Soon after it

was rebuilt for the second time, Wright was evicted as the result of bankruptcy, and found himself homeless. His second marriage to a woman who became mentally deranged proved disastrous, and she pursued him outrageously as he sought to dissolve the union. Together with the woman who would become his third wife, he was arrested on charges of violating the Mann Act and briefly jailed. Through it all he persevered, focusing attention on those few commissions he received during the 1920s and conceiving new prototypes that he would continue to explore for the remainder of his career.[2] He approached the design of large complexes with expanded vision, exploring unusual technologies and untried geometries, and effecting unparalleled unifications of buildings, roadways, and terrain, so that a new landscape emerged, one in which the underlying patterns of each setting were revealed through human intervention. Auldbrass would come to embody these accomplishments.

In 1928, Wright's troubled second marriage was at last dissolved and he was free to marry Olgivanna Milanoff, with whom he had already fathered a child, but whose own divorce from an earlier husband had been complicated.[3] Domestic tranquility began to be re-established, yet commissions were still very few, and many people assumed his career to be over. In 1932, still lacking work, Wright and his third wife established the Taliesin Fellowship, and the community of apprentices provided needed support, both financial and professional. In that same year, for the Willey house commission, he initiated the first of what would become a long series of relatively small, affordable homes aimed at a broad segment of the population. Then in the mid 1930s came two commissions that would catapult Wright back to the acknowledged forefront of his profession: Fallingwater (the Edgar Kaufmann house, Mill Run, Pennsylvania, 1934) and the S. C. Johnson & Son Administration Building (Racine, Wisconsin, 1936). Wright never lacked for work again.

By 1938, when he was first contacted by Stevens, Wright was involved in at least twenty commissions, including several houses, a vast scheme of interconnected buildings for Florida Southern College (Lakeland, Florida, 1938 ff), and a civic center complex known as Monona Terrace (Madison, Wisconsin, 1938; a reworked version was completed in 1997). He was continuing to expand Taliesin and beginning to build a second home and office complex, Taliesin West, near Scottsdale, Arizona. His involvement with his own estates may well have made the Auldbrass commission one of particular interest—as some have suggested, almost a vision of what he might have built for himself in that third and significantly different climate.[4]

During the next two years, while he was designing the first portions of Auldbrass, Wright received nearly fifty more commissions, including, in addition to more houses, a monumental urban complex known as Crystal Heights

(Washington, D.C., 1939, unbuilt). With his work again widely published, and his writings, and with unending requests for lectures and special appearances, he was enjoying fame as no other architect of the time. Thus, while he was conceiving his first and only southern plantation, Wright himself could be described as a force of nature with which to be reckoned, and even so powerful a man as Leigh Stevens treated him with deference as they worked together to realize Auldbrass.

Stevens's first meeting with Wright took place at Taliesin in late November or early December, 1938. He wrote to Wright on December 18 of that year to remind him of their recent discussion of the proposed commission, and he promised to send pictures of the property after he next visited the site.[5] Stevens's business had continued to expand; he wrote from the Baltimore office of the C. L. Stevens Company, and he had dropped by Taliesin with no formal appointment during one of his frequent business trips.

As to how Stevens chose Wright, there are no exact explanations. His daughter believes he had known of Wright for many years as a result of seeing the Meyer May house (1908) in Grand Rapids, Michigan, not far from his hometown of Muskegon. Other members of his family lived only a few blocks from the May house, and together with his parents, Stevens had visited Grand Rapids several times while growing up.[6]

Whatever his childhood memories, it seems unlikely that anyone with Stevens's knowledge of business and property could not have known of Wright, given the widespread publicity Wright was then receiving, with accounts featured in such journals as *Life* and *The New Yorker*.[7] In January of 1938, he had even appeared on the cover of *Time*.[8] From such obvious sources, Stevens may well have been drawn to the special issue of *Architectural Forum* dedicated to Wright's work, and that issue, too, had also appeared in January 1938.[9] In that issue, Taliesin was the first building featured (following a table of contents with a photograph and brief mention of the Cheney house). It was described as "a house of the north," emphasized as a self-sufficient development, and illustrated with photographs and plans showing extensive farm buildings. Herbert Johnson's home, Wingspread, was also included in the issue, and again presented as part of a working farm.[10]

Although not revealing how he first heard of Wright, Stevens later explained that he believed him to be "the greatest living architect" and "wanted to give that genius full range." Continuing, he claimed that he selected Wright "because the South was a challenge,"[11] almost as if he wanted a southern counterpart to the *Forum*'s description of Taliesin as the "house of the north." Stevens sought to build a plantation that was the "best of all of them, but . . .

OPPOSITE
FIG. 25
PRELIMINARY SITE PLAN
Auldbrass. FLWA 4015.001

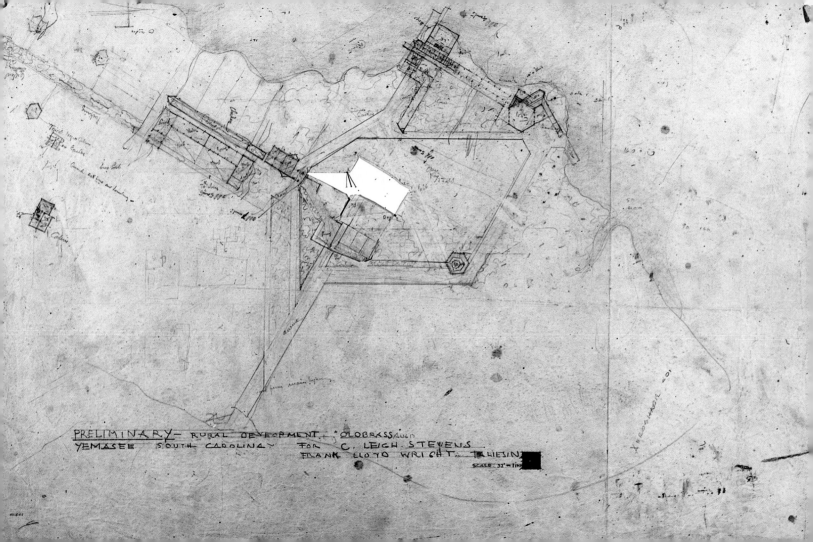

PRELIMINARY – RURAL DEVELOPMENT. "OLOBRASS"
YEMASSEE SOUTH CAROLINA FOR C. LEIGH STEVENS
FRANK LLOYD WRIGHT. TALIESIN
SCALE 32' = 1 inch

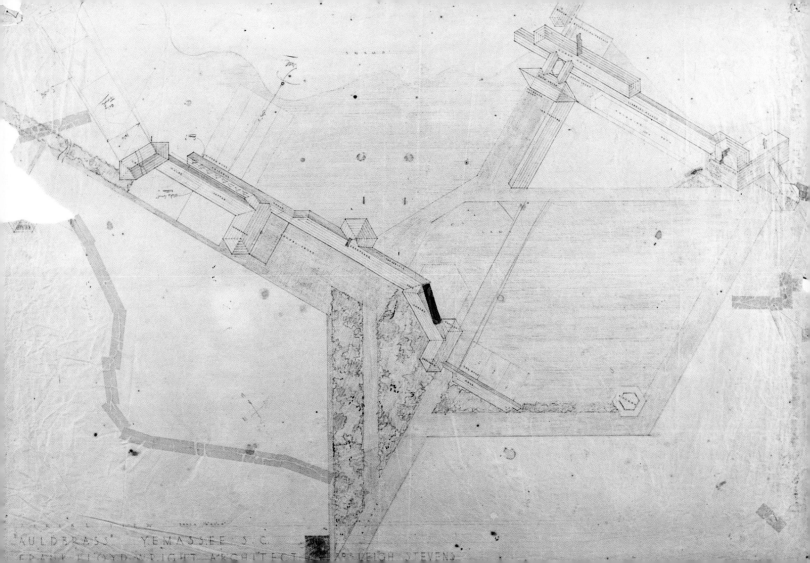

"KULDERAS" YEMASSEE S C
FRANK FLOYD WRIGHT ARCHITECT ... LEIGH STEVENS

totally different."[12] He wanted a fully working farm, complete with dairy, with which he could experiment, but also a place that was to be "a kind of refuge from the pressures and cares of the world . . . a place of rest and work."[13] It can be speculated that Stevens sought to revive the spirit of the ideal plantation, but on twentieth-century terms, as if he were determined to bring his own genius to bear on a seemingly insoluble problem: an efficient and profitable southern plantation dependent not on servitude, but instead made workable by well-paid and comfortably accommodated labor. As Stevens later recalled, he gave Wright unlimited freedom to work with him in conceiving this new approach; "I made some suggestions," he related, "but no demands, financial or otherwise."[14]

It took longer than Stevens expected to get photographs of his property for Wright to examine. As he explained in a second letter, dated April 3, 1939, it had first been necessary to clear timber and underbrush from the area where he intended to build.[15] He enclosed a rough sketch that he had made of the site and briefly referred to the program he had discussed with Wright during their meeting several months earlier. His confidence in Wright seemed strengthened; he wrote, "I remember how very well your home in Wisconsin fitted into the country and I think that if the same fitness could be accomplished here it would give one a sense of having done something very worthwhile."[16] His description of the site that follows in the same letter offers a clear sense of prospect as he perceived it:

> The area covered by the sketch enclosed is a bank which runs approximately parallel to a country road, is almost level and is about 14 feet above the swamp which is flooded most of the time so that water comes right up to the foot of the bank. This bank, being situated as it is between the swamp and the road and being at a higher level than the swamp would, I think, afford the best drainage on the place. It varies in width from 200 to 500 feet and it is my present idea to devote this entire area to the main house and gardens. Concerning the various elements of the place such as dogs, horses, caretaker's house, etc., it seems to me best to put these units on the bank which extends for about 2 miles along the road (outside of the area sketched). . . .

Reportedly, Stevens also sent Wright two books on plantations: *Old South: A Carolina Rice Plantation of the Fifties* by Alice Ravenel Huger Smith, and *Prince Williams Parish and Plantations* by Frances Marion Hutson and John R.

RIGHT
FIG. 27
PLAN AND ELEVATION OF MAIN HOUSE AND GUEST HOUSE
Auldbrass. FLWA 4015.002

FOLLOWING PAGES
FIG. 28
MAIN HOUSE FROM LAKE
Auldbrass. Paul Rocheleau, 2003

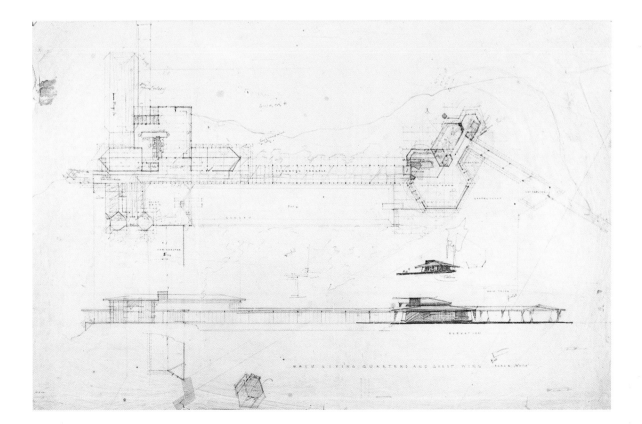

FIG. 29
REV. THOMAS E. LEDBETTER HOUSE
411 Bayard Street, Beaufort, S.C., ca.
1800/1840. Historic American Buildings Survey,
HABS SC, 7-Beauf, 9-1; Prints and Photographs Division,
Library of Congress

OPPOSITE
FIG. 30
DRAYTON HALL
Near Charleston, S.C., ca.1738–42.
Ben Judah Lubschec, photographer. From Samuel
Gaillard Stoney, *Plantations of the Carolina Low
Country*, Charleston: Carolina Art Association/Gibbes
Museum of Art, 1938, 142

Todd.[17] Images of a traditional sort (similar to those in other publications) dominate the latter (fig. 30), and perhaps in part Stevens sent this book to show what he did not want, to judge by his later statements. Images of Tara, the idealized southern plantation depicted in the movie version of "Gone With the Wind"—released in 1939, while Wright was beginning his design—would have been even better known (fig. 13).

Other images in Smith's book emphasize qualities of the local landscape, and further remind how axial organization, as a traditional element of some plantations, could work to advantage to unify building with place (fig. 32). A very few of the pictures contained within emphasize a lush exoticism of landscape with buildings seen as an informal adjunct (fig. 31), as do the impressionistic watercolors in Smith's book. These, it could be speculated, offered more tangible points of departure for Wright's design. Because there were few, if any, antebellum survivors in the immediate vicinity of Stevens's property, there were no closer models that Wright might have considered. Houses in nearby Beaufort at best suggest a regional pattern, with long, low, open, thin-columned, two-story porches extending across their fronts (fig. 29). If one were

to demand some quality that Wright might have drawn from these, it would probably be their sense of an open, permeable perimeter.

Wright's earliest known drawing for Auldbrass is dated July 23, 1939 (fig. 25). Labeled "Preliminary Rural Development, Oldbrass," it reflects a close reading of Stevens letter, with the main house, guest house, and gardens located along the bank near the imagined edge of the water, and with the other buildings—kennels, stables, caretaker's house, and staff cabins—placed further back, but in a loosely parallel line, with cabins to be continued beyond the boundary of the sketch, utilizing land that Stevens had indicated. The building elements incorporate loosely hexagonal shapes, and they are joined by continuous roofs into two primary groupings, with a single hexagonal pavilion shown midway between the two, and with hexagonal cabins extending to the left. Roadways that link these elements augment the hexagonal geometry and complete the loosely unified composition.

Typical of Wright's approach, the layout shown remained essentially unchanged as he developed the proj-

ect. Much, if not all, of the sketch appears to be in his hand, and if his method conformed to what he consistently claimed, and what has been shown to be the case in his design of Fallingwater, it was his first sketch for the commission, recording basic concepts for his apprentices to develop.[18] Also typical of Wright's approach was his use of completed drawings to indicate future modifications. Thus certain notes that he later added to the drawing served as instructions to his apprentices, no doubt recording the results of later discussions with Stevens, as will be discussed.

Stevens's reaction, recorded in a letter of August 14, 1939, was favorable. "I do like your Old Brass layouts very much," he wrote, and added (somewhat optimistically) that he wanted to start building in the fall.[19] He promised to send an accurate survey and supplied additional details regarding his program. There were to be forty dogs, a small house for himself with two bedrooms and one room for hunting apparel, and "a Negro cabin . . . [the] present standard is a square or rectangular cabin."

Four letter-sized pages of notes in Wright's hand, taped together so they suggest a sort of diagram, record these specific elements of the program together with other items that may have been communicated by telephone or recalled from an earlier meeting.[20] These notes record significant refinements of the program and show Wright's attention to clients' requests. Elements to be added include a swimming pool, which is not shown in the drawing of July 23, but which appears in drawings that follow. Kennels for 40 dogs are noted; perhaps these were more extensive than Wright had first thought, helping account for a later modification outlined on the July 23 drawing, in which the element containing the kennels was moved further from the house by cutting it from the original sheet and flipping it back (as may be seen by the lacunae, fig. 25). The cabins, too, may have been added to that drawing, or at least the single square cabin reflecting the description in Stevens's letter, which is at odds with the other shapes of the composition. Also added to the July 23 drawing is a light pencil notation, "Auld", over "Old," and indeed, beginning with the next drawings, Wright would firmly label the project "Auldbrass." Stevens remembered the variation of the name as Wright's invention, and came to accept it.[21]

Clearly the plantation was growing in scope. Additional program elements listed in the separate pages

of notes include stalls for fifteen horses and mules, places for five milk cows and perhaps 500 chickens. These numbers are in keeping with the developed plans that followed. Mr. Stevens's "small cottage" is noted as being for a bachelor (he had separated from his first wife in 1934). By contrast, the commodious guest house was to incorporate a special gun room and accommodate at least fifteen people. Separate housing was needed for a manager, noted as "white" with a wife and two children, and a laundry and bath house was required for the staff, who were to be housed in cabins of their own.

Stevens, assuming the staff would be largely African American, referred to them in the parlance of the day as Negroes, and the use of the terms "Negro" and "white" to differentiate hierarchies of employees continued intermittently throughout the period of design and construction. While troubling today, these terms reflect attitudes common for the time. Probably neither Stevens nor Wright were aware of the prejudicial stance such terms implied, and probably neither intended any injustice. In the discussion that follows, I have chosen to substitute "staff" for "Negro" to more neutrally reflect assignments and functions.

On his program notes, Wright had recorded a projected cost of $50,000. Given the positive outlook both men had regarding budgets, it is possible this relatively modest amount was expected to cover everything, and it is, in fact, not radically less than the initially contracted price of $84,537.66, as described in Chapter 4. Wright was bringing in modestly sized Usonian houses about the size of the "cottage" for under $10,000,[22] and considering the simplified construction he envisioned, together with the minimal plumbing and heating requirements for many of the service buildings, he almost certainly thought it attainable. Eventually, Stevens spent more than $250,000 building Auldbrass; the final figure is not known—Stevens claimed he stopped keeping accurate records after that point.[23]

Long before those expenses were incurred, Stevens waited impatiently for the developed architectural drawings that would allow him to begin construction. In late October 1939, he asked if he might come to Taliesin to collect them; Wright replied, "Sorry to say not enough ready."[24] In November Stevens cabled, "Am planning to come to see you Sunday. Do hope you are ready. I am getting worried for fear you will get to Arizona and I will be homeless and planless too."[25] This time it was Wright's special assistant, Eugene Masselink, who answered that "Mr. Wright's plans are not yet made. . . ."[26] During this time the payment of architectural fees also figured in their correspondence, with Stevens's impatience for completed drawings now matched by Wright's for money.[27]

At least three drawings in the Frank Lloyd Wright Archives seem to reflect the progress Wright reported during the fall and winter of 1939–40. In what appears to be the first (fig. 27), the main house and guest house are shown in the same relationship as in the earlier site plan (see fig. 25), but at larger scale and with greater detail. A newly added swimming pool now parallels the open pergola linking the two buildings, and the walls of the main house are inclined while those of the guest house are vertical. The compact, fully hexagonal plan of the main house includes a small kitchen (or "workspace") opening off one corner of the living room, and, at the opposite side, an open car shelter linked to the house by a roofed connection. Elsewhere on the drawing are a diagrammatic plan and elevation of the staff cabin.[28] The other two drawings show the main house alone, with the plan drafted over a hexagonal grid.[29] The living room is given a more complicated shape, and outward-opening hinged panels, taking the place of conventional doors, are indicated as being covered in canvas.

By mid-January 1940, the completed set of promised drawings was ready. Wright cabled Stevens, "Have your plans with me. Very happy concerning them. In Boston 23rd, 24th, 25th. Would like to present plans to you myself. Can't go to Yemassee this time. Where most convenient to you to meet."[30] Where they met or when is not made clear in the ensuing correspondence, but the drawings, dated January 10, 1940, are very clear indeed.

Two drawings of the presentation set show the entire development: a roof plan (fig. 26) and an aerial perspective (fig. 23). The individual units have been more clearly defined than in the earlier site plan, but without loss of sweeping unity. In the plan, the main house at the upper right is joined by a long pergola and swimming pool to the larger guest house at the left. Each relates directly to the imagined shoreline of what has been labeled "swamp." On a parallel axis with this grouping, an even more extended line of farm buildings, again linked by continuous roofs, unfolds more informally. The kennels at the lower end join at right angles to a transverse element housing a cook shed and saddle room, which is joined in turn to an angled element containing stalls for the horses. Re-establishing the parallel line of the main house and guest house, the long element at the center was to contain a car shed adjacent to the horse stalls, then a caretaker's house with a projecting hexagonal bay facing the shoreline. The element projecting at right angles from the back of the caretaker's house was intended as a workshop, open to the partially enclosed gravel court where service vehicles were to be parked. Two closely spaced pavilions extend beyond: the upper to house chickens, and the lower to house cattle and mules. A large, angled barn lies at the end of this nearly 500-foot long grouping.

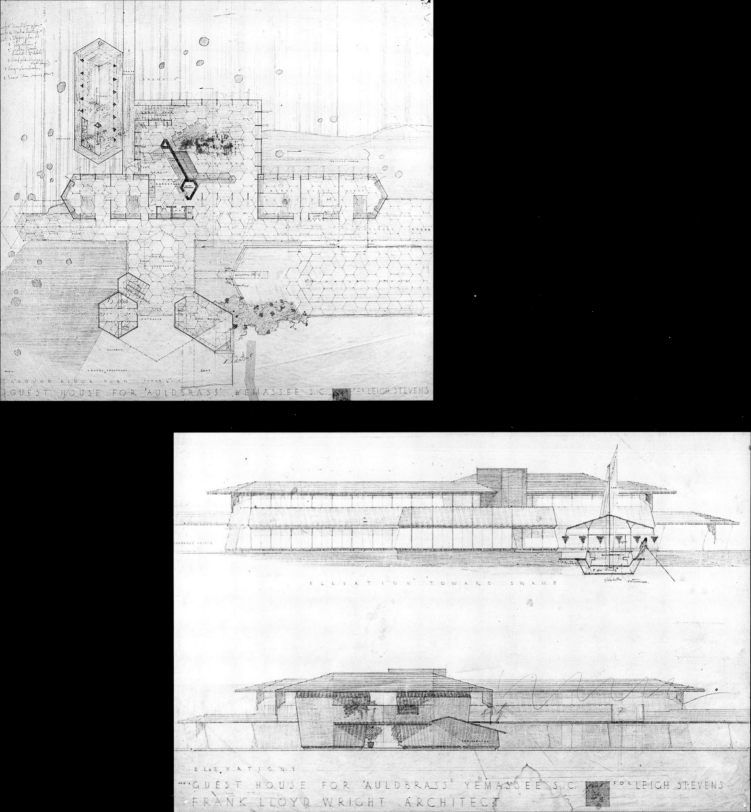

GROUND FLOOR PLAN

GUEST HOUSE FOR 'AULDBRASS' YEMASSEE S.C. FOR LEIGH STEVENS

ELEVATION TOWARD SWAMP

ELEVATIONS

GUEST HOUSE FOR 'AULDBRASS' YEMASSEE S.C. FOR LEIGH STEVENS
FRANK LLOYD WRIGHT ARCHITECT

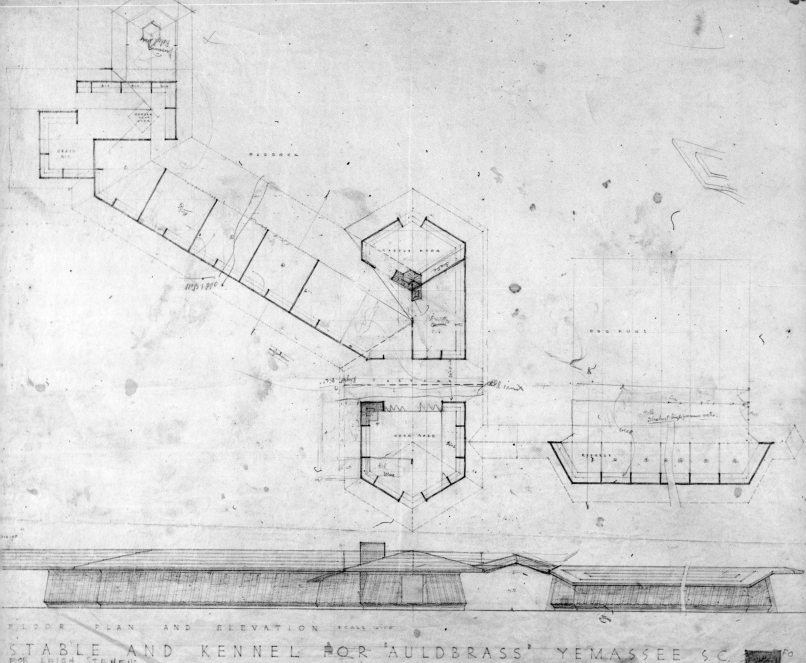

FLOOR PLAN AND ELEVATION SCALE

STABLE AND KENNEL FOR 'AULDBRASS' YEMASSEE S.C.
FOR LEIGH STEVENS
FRANK LLOYD WRIGHT ARCHITECT. FOR LEIGH STEVENS

Gravel driveways shown on the plan establish secondary lines of connection, meant to be embanked by planted esplanades and to penetrate the connecting roofs of the farm buildings at selected locations. An isolated, hexagonal pavilion at the lower right, originally intended as an aviary, forms a pivot in the overall composition, marking the bend in the main roadway as it approaches the house. The aerial perspective is cast too high to show this element, but staff cabins extending along the line of the bank are visible, a last sequence of elements establishing unity at great scale.

Additional drawings of this set amplify individual elements. In the plan and elevation of the main house (fig. 40), angled walls support broad overhangs, and each corner of the overhangs is articulated by a richly detailed copper downspout that hovers above the flat surface of the ground, so the entire roof seems almost to float. Wright envisioned the house itself as positioned at the edge of a relatively steep bank, with stairs leading down to the surface of the water. In actuality he had misjudged the site, as later came to light.

The guest house, as rendered, engaged even more dramatically with the shoreline, for its living room formed an embankment that appeared to project into the water; and at the upper left corner, a sumptuous, hexagonal dining barge sits poised for some elegant banquet, when it might float gently away, under the oak trees and Spanish moss, toward the Combahee river (fig. 34). Adding to the sense of leisured ease are a bath house and gun room, placed in hexagonal pavilions adjacent to the entrance where they would form an impressive gateway. Additional facilities were located on an upper floor of the hexagonal pavilions, joined by a bridge across an open court to a long line of guest rooms over the living and dining areas below. A terrace adjoining the bedrooms was to overlook the marshy wetlands beyond.

While Wright employed hexagonal geometry throughout the composition, he varied its application so that differences among parts can be perceived, and so that a range of spatial qualities would result. Thus the plan of the guest house, combining hexagonal and rectangular elements, differs from the plan of the main house, which is fully hexag-

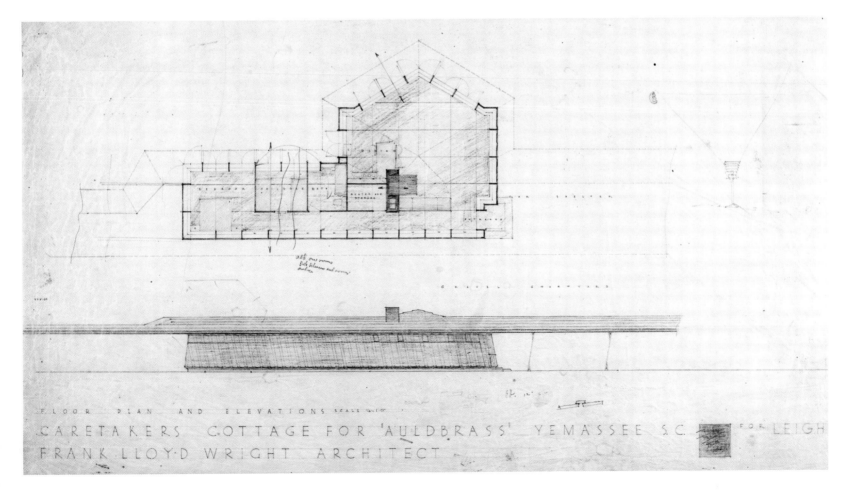

CARETAKERS COTTAGE FOR 'AULDBRASS' YEMASSEE S.C. FOR LEIGH
FRANK LLOYD WRIGHT ARCHITECT

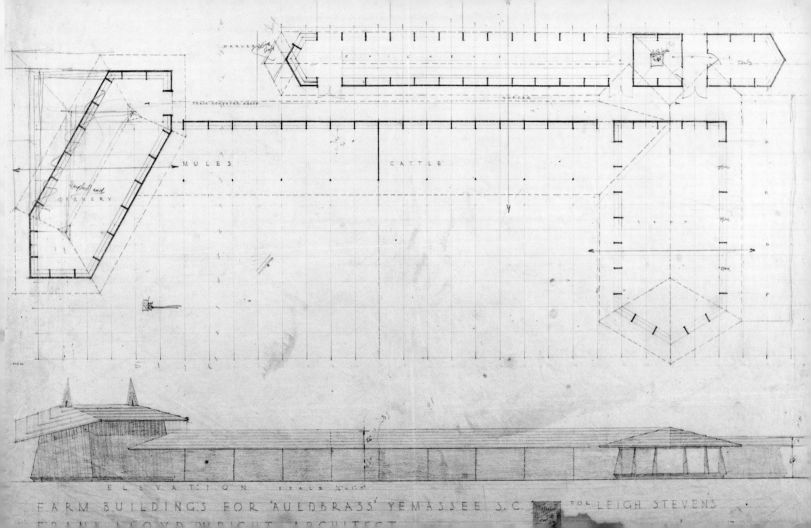

MULES   CATTLE

GRANERY

ELEVATION

FARM BUILDINGS FOR 'AULDBRASS' YEMASSEE S.C. FOR LEIGH STEVENS
FRANK LLOYD WRIGHT ARCHITECT

onal. Similar variations can be detected in the elevations, for the walls of the guest house cant in both directions below their broad, overhanging eaves (fig. 35), while those of the main house angle consistently inward. In the farm buildings, too, Wright modified the hexagonal module in ways that provided flexibility of arrangement as well as distinctive spatial character. In his presentation drawings of 1940, the angled boards of the canted walls and the continuous horizontality of the low roofs are firmly rendered, and the individual elements are persuasively joined. The main roadway to the guest house was to pass under a low gable linking the kennels with the cook shed, providing a framed view toward the buildings lying beyond (fig. 36).[31] The caretaker's house reads almost as a detached dwelling, but for the continuous roofs that incorporate it into the unified grouping (fig. 37). Clustered together in the most distant segment are the farm buildings themselves, with the elevation showing more convincingly than the aerial perspective how firmly the barn (sometimes indicated as a

granary, sometimes as a hay barn)—its taller height amplified by roof-top ventilators—was to terminate the composition (fig. 39).

A final drawing dated January 10, 1940, shows the staff cabin (fig. 43). A simple hexagon in plan, it was to contain a combined living and cooking area together with a partitioned alcove for sleeping. Both spaces were to open through canvas flaps to a large screened porch that wrapped around two sides. There hammocks would provide a cool place for sleeping during the summer. Along a back wall were simple sanitary facilities; bathing was to be provided by a central bathhouse and plunge pool that had yet to be designed. The wall section shown for the cabin was to be essentially the section used throughout the complex: angled board walls supported against sloping stanchions, with continuous ventilating panels to be located at the bottom and at the top. The cabin was to be roofed with bands of copper foil (the threat of a spreading world war had led to restrictions on building materials, and sheet cop-

OPPOSITE
FIG. 39
**PLAN AND ELEVATION
OF FARM BUILDINGS**
Auldbrass. FLWA 4015.008

RIGHT
FIG. 40
**PLAN AND ELEVATION
OF MAIN HOUSE.**
Auldbrass. FLWA 4015.007

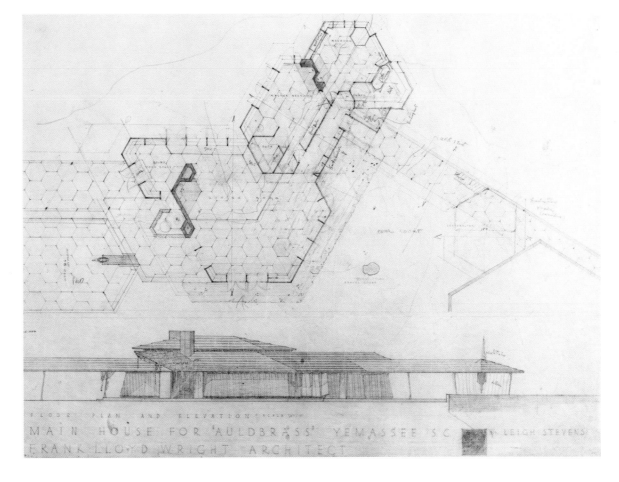

FLOOR PLAN AND ELEVATION
MAIN HOUSE FOR 'AULDBRASS' YEMASSEE S C LEIGH STEVENS
FRANK LLOYD WRIGHT ARCHITECT

per was not available). As with the house and guest house, elaborate copper downspouts at the corners, fully as sculptural as traditional gargoyles, were to provide points of decorative elegance. The wood to be used had yet to be chosen; in his drawing Wright had suggested red cedar, but ultimately a better quality wood was selected.

As Stevens studied the drawings, doubts arose as to the feasibility of using canvas flaps with wood stretchers in place of more conventional glass and wood-framed doors. Wright urged that he visit Taliesin West "to see how canvas looks and works."[32] By April 21, while still doubtful about the canvas, Stevens accepted the rest of Wright's design: "have spent many hours over your plans and suggestions are practically nil."[33] He soon specified these alterations, and they were indeed relatively minor: another bedroom in the caretaker's house, modest enlargements to the chicken houses and the workshop, and the relocation of the kitchen from the main house to a separate pavilion, connected by a screen porch, to "restore the living room to your original design which seems to be about perfect."[34] These changes Wright duly noted on the January 10, 1940, drawings and incorporated in later versions. He converted the car shelter of the main house to the detached kitchen Stevens had requested and made the former workspace into a study. Further—perhaps to guarantee that its original spirit be retained—he enlarged the plan of the house by one modular unit. While enlarging the chicken coops he also moved them further from the cattle and mule barn, creating an internal court that would provide better light and air for the adjacent buildings. The additional bedroom was added to the caretaker's house by lengthening it within its roofed enclosure.

Stevens planned to build the farm buildings first, together with five or six staff cabins, and he wanted to begin as quickly as possible.[35] Yet an impending divorce from his first wife delayed the beginning of construction. The decree would become final on July 2, 1941, but by the spring of 1940, it had become clear that Stevens would lose his house and adjoining property in the Boston suburb of Westwood as part of the legal settlement. His daughter recalled that he was embittered by this loss and wished to protect himself from any future claims that might result from a future marriage or other entanglement.[36] Given the complexities of his business operations and of his original acquisition of the Auldbrass property, there were no doubt other concerns regarding the future status of his projected investment. Thus Stevens delayed the beginning of construction long enough to secure the establishment of the Auldbrass Trust, an entity that would protect his property from any future claim. Negotiations leading to its formation had actually begun in 1938, and issues relating to its legal status were not fully resolved until 1941, but activity was most intense during the spring of 1940, when Stevens and his attorneys were securing court rulings.[37] Ever sensitive to his own needs, Wright inquired if he might arrange for similar protection of his own property.[38]

In his legal negotiations, Stevens was represented by no less a figure than Joseph N. Welch, of the Boston firm Hale and Dorr. Welch was later to become famous as the Army counsel in the Army-McCarthy hearings in 1954. Welch and Stevens were close friends, as correspondence shows, and Welch would become a frequent guest at Auldbrass. As he was later to write, "I don't think you ever came anywhere near understanding how utterly delightful my four trips to South Carolina were," thanking Stevens in particular for the cooking, the hunting, and the backgammon games.[39] It would be several years before Auldbrass was ready to receive such guests as Welch, but by the spring of 1940 its design was essentially set.

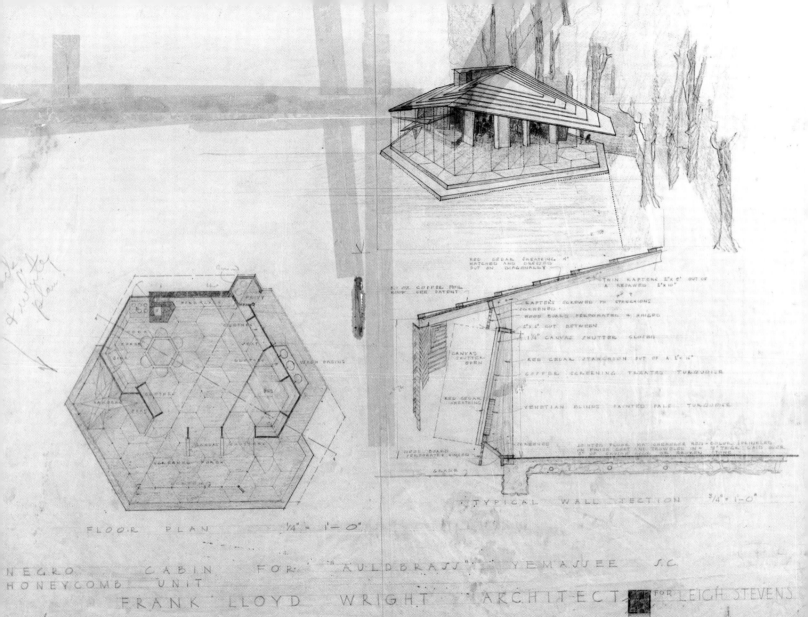

FLOOR PLAN   1/4" = 1'-0"

TYPICAL WALL SECTION   3/4" = 1'-0"

NEGRO CABIN FOR "AULDBRASS" YEMASSEE S.C.
HONEYCOMB UNIT

FRANK LLOYD WRIGHT ARCHITECT FOR LEIGH STEVENS

CHAPTER 3

GEOMETRIC INVENTION IN THE SHAPING OF AULDBRASS

With Auldbrass, as earlier noted, Wright reconfigured the image of a southern plantation as surely as he reconfigured all conventional forms that engaged his attention. He eliminated references to formal symmetry that had traditionally elevated the planter's residence to a visibly dominating position, instead conceiving a continuous, angled enclosure about multiple axes that defined no center, no fixed position of ruling authority. The house itself, smaller in scale and lower in overall profile than the related farm buildings, undifferentiated by material or form, became instead an extension of those farm buildings that were to provide for its economic support. Gone was the grand allee of the traditional plantation, the single, major roadway that reinforced hierarchical order by focusing on one grand entrance. In its place Wright substituted variously angled driveways of changing direction; they would approach, then penetrate, the outer line of farm buildings. These farm buildings would seem magnified by this device as they, in turn, framed views to the main house beyond.

Arriving at the house by automobile, one would stop within a gently scaled parking court adjacent to an unprepossessing door. Similar to many of Wright's designs for country houses, there was no single, obvious entrance. Instead, through an indirect route, one was made to experience a part of the place itself before entering; and other ways of entering also became apparent, so that social order seemed ever more relaxed. Of large-scale formal

plantings there were to be none, except for cultivated fields of the working farm that lay beyond immediate view. Instead, within the expansive ambit of the house, existing local species alone were to be retained, modified only by selective thinning. Wright planned to restrict cultivated plantings to small, geometrically defined beds arranged to form a transitional band between large, open areas surrounding the house and the house itself. These beds were to be filled with flowering shrubs, massed informally within their boundaries to augment the sense of continuous, informal unity. In these and other ways, the rigid architectural frame of the traditional southern plantation, one that had reinforced a private and autocratic world, gave way to a more humane and democratic order.

Within another frame of reference, Auldbrass embodies Wright's theory of organic architecture. This complicated and evolving philosophy of design constitutes a study in itself, defying easy explanation, but critical aspects can at least be summarized.[1] In sympathy with his Unitarian background, it can be argued that Wright honored the visible unity of things as a manifestation of larger order, feeling that unity was implicit in all aspects of life, and he believed that it lay with the architect to identify and clarify those patterns. Sympathetic also to Transcendentalist thinking, he saw humankind as a noble part of nature, and not in opposition to it.[2] He considered buildings to be a natural extension of human process, and hence themselves an expression of nature, reinforcing connections between people and their world, and of individuals to their specific locales in that world. Consistently he thought in terms of universal ideals and architectural prototypes. These were not ideals or prototypes of an incorporeal sort, dealing with concepts of pure form detached from worldly place. Instead universality was sought through linkages of humankind to place, and place to cosmos, so that patterns implicit in specific sites were made into visible components of the grander order they supported. Thus could life itself be meaningfully enriched through architecture. Nowhere was this more fervently sought than at Auldbrass.

The means that Wright employed to amplify qualities of place, and to effect a broad and nurturing unity, depended very much on his manipulation of geometry. Euclidian order lay at the core of his envisaged world, as it had in so much rationalist thinking of the nineteenth century. Yet he was able to vary the standard shapes of square, triangle, and circle with ravishing results, so that Euclidian order became infused with a richness largely unapproached by other architects. Again Auldbrass stands as a paradigmatic example, for its design depends only in part on simple modular shapes, shapes that Wright himself exploited to extract every possible nuance of architectural expression. How those shapes might reflect the nature of a

specific place is more difficult to understand, although possibilities will be suggested in the discussion that follows.

In his writings, Wright consistently attributed his early fascination with geometry to the Froebel toys that his mother had given him as a child. Much has been written of this kindergarten system designed to foster a sense of universal order in the child.[3] Certainly the Euclidian shapes of the cut papers and various block-like elements, and the evenly-gridded table upon which they were to be arranged in expression of unifying patterns, accord with Wright's later designs. In his autobiography he recalled,

> That early kindergarten experience with the straight line; the flat plane; the square; the triangle; the circle! If I wanted more, the square modified by the triangle gave the hexagon—the circle modified by the straight line would give the octagon. Adding thickness, getting 'sculpture' thereby, the square became the cube, the triangle the tetrahedron, the circle the sphere. These primary forms and figures were the secret of all effects . . . .[4]

The belief that all forms in nature could be reduced to simple geometries, that such geometries provided limitless means for the architect to manipulate, and that through their orderly, systematic manipulation designs could be made expressive of larger truths—all seem to derive from Wright's ongoing interpretations of the Froebel toys. He wrote of these toys,

> the exciting cardboard shape . . . . Smooth triangular shapes. . .cut in rhomboids with which to make designs on the flat tabletop. What shapes they made naturally if only you would let them! . . . Shapes that lay hidden behind the appearances all about. . . . Here was something for invention to seize and use to create.[5]

In practice, Wright worked with various Euclidian shapes, favoring no single system. To observers, his use of triangular geometries was particularly striking. His fascination with variations inherent in this shape may have been encouraged by the writings of Eugène-Emmanuel Violet-Le-Duc (1814–1879), the great nineteenth-century French rationalist whose writings Wright consistently praised. Not atypically for the time, Violet-Le-Duc emphasized unity as an essential element of design, saying at one point, "art must be regarded as an indivisible unity . . . ".[6] Also reflecting nineteenth-century rationalism, Viollet-Le-Duc, like Wright, sought honest expressions of materials and structure; he damned the cutting of stone to imitate smaller joint patterns, for example, as "a lie in stone . . . it will not be the expression of the nature of the materials employed . . .".[7] He identified geometry as fundamental to architecture,[8] and he singled out the equilateral triangle for special praise. He believed the triangle "most satisfies the

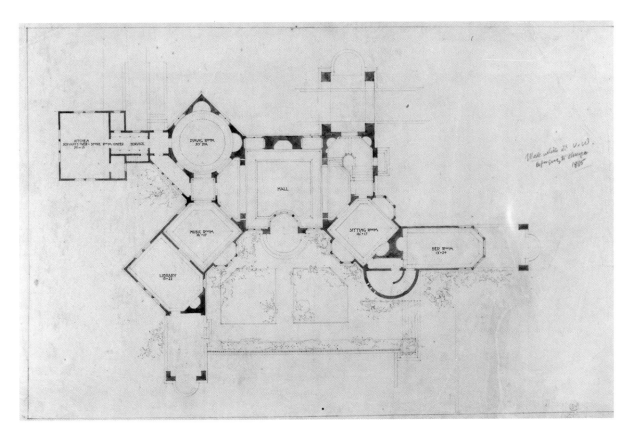

eye . . .", not only because of its representative equalities of line and angle, but also for its relationship to the hexagon, which, through superimposition, subdivides the circumference of the circle into six equal parts. Continuing, he wrote, "There is no geometrical figure which conveys greater satisfaction to the mind, none which better fulfills those conditions of stability and regularity which appeal most agreeably to the eye and mind."[9] He went so far as to relate the equilateral triangle to the pointed arch, ". . . the point of departure for an entirely new system of construction . . . in France in the twelfth century."[10]

While English versions of Viollet-le-Duc's writings such as *Discourses on Architecture* were readily available to Wright, the ten-volume *Dictionnaire Raisonné de L'Architecture* had not appeared in translated form except for an obscure manuscript translated by Nathan Clifford Ricker. Whether Wright knew of this or not, or whether he read later excerpts of Ricker's translation published from 1927 to 1930, is not known, although he claimed to be familiar with the *Dictionnaire*, and at the very least he could have looked at its illustrations. But it is unlikely that he could have read the entry on "Style," in which Viollet-le-Duc posited that the earth's crust, in cooling, had been stabilized by crystalline variations of the equilateral triangle, so that its first layer—granite—was uniquely composed of juxtaposed rhomboids.[11] A diagram of this layer parallels in the most general sense Wright's later modular experiments, and Viollet-le-Duc's suggestion that such pattern lay beneath surfaces of the earth provides an equally parallel rationale for its employment as a planning device.

However Wright came to his own fascination with triangular shapes and their variants, he first used them conservatively. Like many architects of his day, he angled wings of his buildings and incorporated such angular elements as octagonal pavilions and half-octagonal bays into his layouts, but such elements were always subservient to a dominant pattern of orthogonal order. His early design for the Henry N. Cooper house (La Grange, Illinois, 1890, unbuilt) is typical in this regard (fig. 47), as is the octagonal study added to his Oak Park home and studio in 1895. An early use of the hexagon appears in a plan of the Francis W. Little house (Peoria, Illinois, 1903), but again it is treated as an adjunct to an orderly plan, adding subtle variation without challenging conventional order. This parallels the manner in which hexagonal shapes had been used, however sparingly, throughout history, as in the fore-

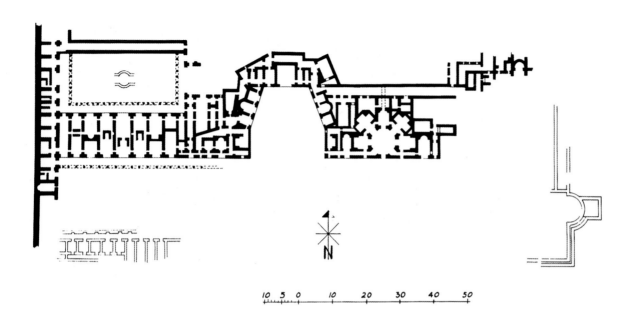

court of the Sanctuary at Baalbek (begun in the early first century and completed some two centuries later) or the palace at Stupinigi, near Turin (1729–33), by Filippo Juvarra. In these, as in Wright's Little house, the hexagon tended to be employed as a complete shape, without variations of interlocking fragments.

Closer in spirit to Wright's later exploitation of triangular geometries were villas built during the Roman Empire, such as the expansive, elegantly appointed Domus Aurea of Nero (A.D. 64–68), built within the city of Rome itself (fig. 48).[12] Yet even there, as in the still more famous Villa of Trajan (A.D. 118–138), there is no visible attempt to order space according to an even field of triangular or hexagonal units; instead, elements were brusquely juxtaposed without the more flowing quality that Wright would develop in the twentieth century.

Apparently Wright's first decisive step toward a broader exploration of hexagonal geometry came in 1923, with the Barge for Two (unbuilt), a floating cabin envisioned as one of several prototypes for Lake Tahoe (fig. 49). While the hexagonal units remain individually visible, they are overlapped to enclose subsidiary spaces, and a more complex volumetric play results, with volumes defined by angled rather than orthogonal elements, not unlike Borromini's S. Ivo (Rome, 1642–1650). Further, this geometry carries into the walls themselves, with lapped boards defining angled profiles in elevation. Of the other three barges in this unbuilt project, two also have angled prows, but less fully expressed. The need for the barges to be easily moveable across the surface of Lake Tahoe may well have suggested angular shapes to Wright, but he soon began to incorporate them more fully into other, more stable buildings as well.

Two later projects of the 1920s—the decade when Wright reinvented himself, so to speak, and began to plan more expansively—show his continued exploration of angled geometries and lead toward his design of Auldbrass. Neither was built. The first, a vast desert compound for A. M. Johnson, designed in 1924 for a site along Grapevine Canyon, near Death Valley, resembled Auldbrass in several ways (fig. 50). It was to provide a winter retreat for Johnson, but also operate as a working farm. The service buildings were conceived as an integral part of the complex, unified by low walls (rather than roofs) and related to a connecting network of angled roadways and irrigation channels. The buildings themselves were more conventionally planned than those for Auldbrass, achieving angled relationships through rotation rather than internally angled walls; but like those of Auldbrass they were related to a central pivot—for the Johnson compound, an octagonal chapel rather than a hexagonal aviary. For Johnson, too, the walls of the main house were to be inclined, but by means of corbeled masonry rather than wood frames. As at Auldbrass, the composition of buildings seemed meant to define an otherwise open and

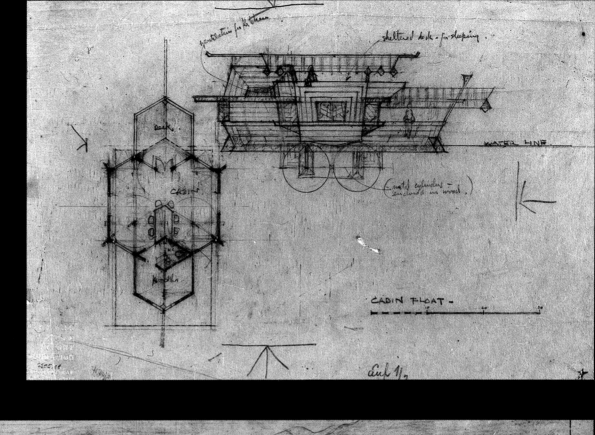

penetration for kitchen

sheltered deck - for sleeping

WATER LINE

(metal cylinders - enclosed in wood.)

DECK

CABIN

KITCHEN

CABIN FLOAT -

Death Valley
A.M. Tolanson - Clips - Dudley. Good line.
Irrigated pets

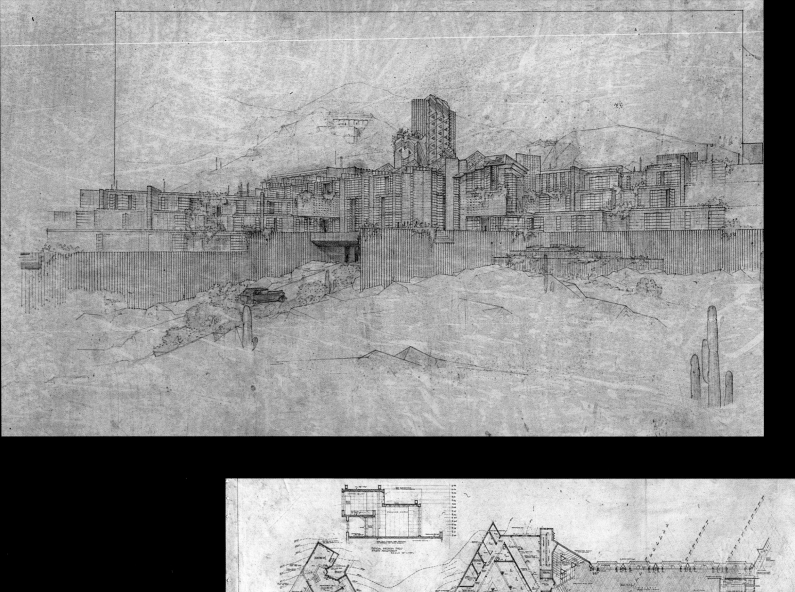

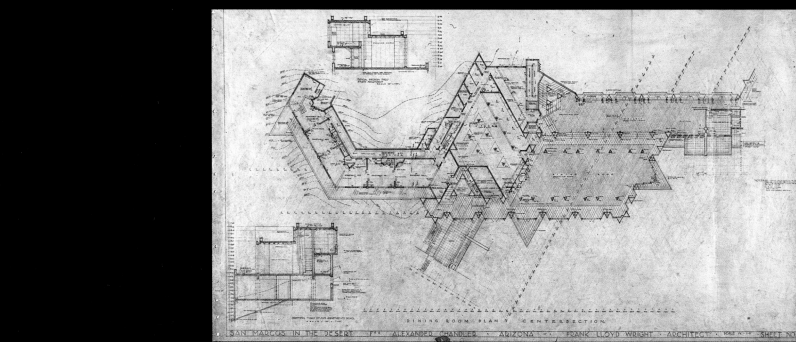

DINING ROOM PLAN ⚘ CENTER SECTION

SAN MARCOS IN THE DESERT · · · ALEXANDER CHANDLER · · ARIZONA · · · FRANK LLOYD WRIGHT · ARCHITECT · · SCALE · · · SHEET Nº

unshaped place, with building materials responsive to locale, for thick masonry walls with relatively few openings work effectively in desert climes.

The second major project of the 1920s to prefigure Auldbrass was the luxurious resort planned for San Marcos in the Desert (near Chandler, Arizona, 1928–29, unbuilt), an even vaster composition of connected units (fig. 52). There Wright exploited angular geometry fully, utilizing a triangular module to shape the central lounges and dining room so that richly faceted spaces would result (fig. 53). Wings containing more conventionally shaped rooms angled out from this central unit; they were to be terraced into the low hill behind and connected by continuous roof terraces. Through architectural intervention, Wright again gave special shape to an otherwise open, largely undifferentiated site. As in the Johnson desert compound, its construction of masonry blocks was conceived in response to its desert climate. This time, however, Wright specifically related his geometry to that of the landscape he perceived. In the special 1938 issue of Architectural Forum devoted to his work, he described his design as:

worked out upon a unit system adapted to the 1-2 or 60-30 triangle because, as you may have noticed, mountain ranges are all 60-30 triangles unless your eye is arrested by an effect produced by one that is equilateral. A cross-section of the talus at the base of the mountains is the hypotenuse of a 30-60 triangle.[13]

In a manner sympathetic to Viollet-le-Duc, he also related the stone of desert settings to buildings themselves:

Stone is the frame on which [man's] Earth is modeled, and wherever it crops out—there the architect may site and learn. . . . As he takes the trail across the great Western Deserts—he may see his buildings—rising in simplicity and majesty from their floors of gleaming sand—where organic life is still struggling for a bare existence; we see them still, as the Egyptians saw and were taught by those they knew. . . . For in the stony bonework of the Earth, the principles that shaped stone as it lies, or as it rises and remains to be sculptured by winds and tide—there sleep forms and styles enough for all the ages, for all of Man.[14]

Other designs of the 1920s also incorporated angled geometries, though in manners less related to Auldbrass. For example, symmetrically grouped hexagonal units in the Steel Cathedral for William Norman Guthrie (New York City, 1927–28, unbuilt) and rotated squares in St. Marks-in-the-Bouwerie apartment tower for William Norman Guthrie (New York City, 1927–31, unbuilt).[15] But the Hanna house of the following decade (Palo Alto, California, 1935–37) emerges as the more immediate pre-

cursor (fig. 54). Wright based its plan on a fully developed hexagonal grid, a unit shape derived from the equilateral triangle (as he had noted with regard to the Froebel toys), and one that could facilitate spatial flexibility. He came to call it a honeycomb system, as first described in 1938:

I am convinced that a cross-section of honeycomb has more fertility and flexibility where human movement is concerned than the square. The obtuse angle is more suited to human 'to and fro' than the right angle. That flow and movement is, in this design, a characteristic lending itself admirably to life, as life is to be lived in it.[16]

This improved quality of movement remained central to his thinking, for the hexagonal module offered ". . .a pattern more natural to human movement. . . . Interiors have more reflex, therefore more response."[17]

The inspiration for this honeycomb system—for Wright's regularization, one might say, of triangular geometries—seems to derive from an apprentice in the Taliesin Fellowship, Cornelia Brierly. She was later married to Peter Berndtson, a fellow apprentice who would supervise the construction of Auldbrass. According to other apprentices, her use of a hexagonal unit in a house she had designed for an aunt was noticed by Wright and soon adapted to his own uses.[18] By identifying the honeycomb as its natural source (he might also have cited the ubiquitous pattern of hexagonal floor tiles), Wright diffused the creative act of discovery. And he would develop the honeycomb module with greater result. Always he emphasized the more relaxed, more flowing sense of space that such gentle angles could engender, angles that he felt more responsive to human use, often using the term "reflexive" to characterize their special qualities.[19]

This same honeycomb unit underlies the floor plan of the main house at Auldbrass. Like the central cluster of public rooms in San Marcos in the Desert, this is the most intensively angled component of the complex. Elsewhere the hexagonal unit is more subdued, with orthogonal units arranged along hexagonal lines, or with combinations of hexagonal and orthogonal shapes. This combination of unit systems—hexagons with overlaid squares—accomplishes at least two things. First, it provides a maximum of planning flexibility. Using the hexagon as a generating shape, six different wall alignments intersecting at five different angles can be accommodated according to the underlying system. This compares with two alignments and one angle in a strictly orthogonal layout, and four alignments and three angles with square units superimposed over an octagonal grid. Second, this combination of unit systems allows Wright to reinforce the importance of the main house. There, the complex, intensively angled yet flowing shapes can be experienced as the culmination of the geometry employed.

With parallel effect, Wright emphasized the central fireplace of the main house in contrast to those elsewhere on the estate so that it assumed special presence. Generously expansive, modular seating was planned so that the entire room seemed almost to suggest a giant Inglenook, a dramatic variation of that traditional element Wright had more often incorporated at smaller scale.[20] Among the many fireplaces at Auldbrass—there were at least ten—this is the only one so treated. In the caretaker's house, the cook shed, and elsewhere, a more linear effect prevails, with the fireplace experienced less centrally. Again Wright amplified geometric patterns in plan—this time through seating elements—to reinforce subtle hierarchies within an intricate complex of related structures.

Obviously such buildings could have been more simply designed, but surely reductive simplicity was never Wright's objective. Rather he sought to express, through selection of a particular grammar of shapes, that "fitness to site" as Stevens had originally requested. This objective Wright consistently pursued—seeking always, it seems, to intensify, through architectural configuration, the experience of place. There were no triangular mountains in the vicinity of Auldbrass—such obvious rationalization had ceased to be a part of his explanations. Instead he said of Auldbrass, "the general plan-form is of a type yielding greatest intimacy with beauty of the surrounding forest-glade."[21] Edgar Kaufmann, jr., later added, "Where in all architecture could one duplicate the casual, competent ease with which these elements are disposed on the land?"[22]

Throughout history, architects have refined square and rectangular modules to extract diverse meanings. During his career, as indicated, Wright expanded this palette to include a diversity of triangular and circular units. Like those before him, his expressive variations of those units were not restricted to plan; rather, in the best of his work, the plan signalled a system that would pervade throughout. Auldbrass provides a fitting example, for the hexagonal units of its plan infused the very shaping of the buildings themselves, establishing a three-dimensional response to the specific qualities of its site that helps explain the original choice of the modular unit involved.

Curtis Besinger, one of Wright's three senior apprentices at the time, worked intermittently on Auldbrass. He recalled how Wright had sketched preliminary plans for the project, but developed the design no further in spite of Stevens's repeated demands for drawings. Preliminary elevations that Besinger and a second senior apprentice, John ("Jack") Howe, attempted to develop failed to engage Wright's attention. Then Wright resolved a fundamental element of his concept, drafting a newly conceived wall section that detailed how the dramatically inclined walls of the preliminary elevations would be achieved. With this fuller crystallization of the hexagonal module accomplished, the distinctive grammar of this particular design became apparent to his apprentices. Working under Wright's re-engaged attention, Besinger and Howe were able to prepare final design drawings according to the grammar now outlined. Clearly the section he developed is critical to a full appreciation of Auldbrass.[23]

Wright's first sketches had shown inclined walls, but without indication as to their construction. The detailed wall section he next conceived gave more specific presence to the design, amplifying qualities of its hexagonal module. It can be seen on the drawing for the staff cabin (see fig. 43), and was later re-drawn for publication (fig. 55). At regular intervals along the concrete slab floors, inclined stanchions were to be positioned on metal brackets, or shoes, with only a portion of their twelve-inch depth resting directly over the slab, and the remainder inclined out over the ground below. This formed a continuous, open slot at the bottom which Wright was to fit with a series of hinged boards that could be opened for ventilation. At the top, canted out to meet the low-sloped roof at ninety degrees, was to be a second row of hinged boards, each embellished with a perforated pattern. Both stanchions and roof rafters were to be exposed inside.

The stanchions were to slope twelve inches inward over a height of about six-and-a-half feet, describing an inward-sloping angle of approximately nine degrees. The single layer of one-inch boards enclosing the spaces inside (also to be left exposed) were to be angled against the frame rather than being attached horizontally, thus strengthening the frame in a manner similar to the hidden diagonal sheathing of conventional frame construction. Here their visible pattern would further amplify the angularity of the design. Continuous wood battens laid beneath the copper foil roofs would provide additional pattern while helping to seal the edges of each successive strip of unfurled roofing. At the corners of the broad overhangs, the geometrically faceted downspouts provided special counterpoint to the walls behind.

The walls were to be assembled with brass screws rather than nails, their slots aligned with the angle of the boards, adding strength as well as elegance to the construction. Selected interior partitions were to be constructed of two thicknesses of boards, counter-angled so that they were self-bracing; the need for internal framing members was thus eliminated. Because such partitions contained no cavities into which wiring could be placed, electrical conduits, where needed, were to be exposed and painted cherokee red.[24] Not that many red conduits were to be required, because the majority of electrical outlets were to be located either along the floor or in the overhead light coves, where their conduits could be concealed.

In those areas of the house where additional ventilation was wanted, as in the stables, but not by means of contin-

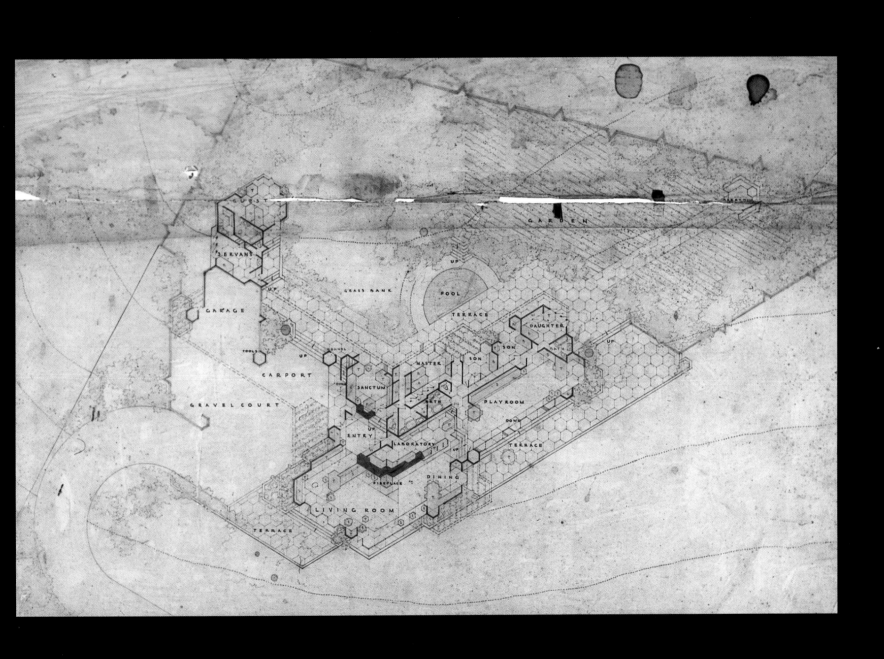

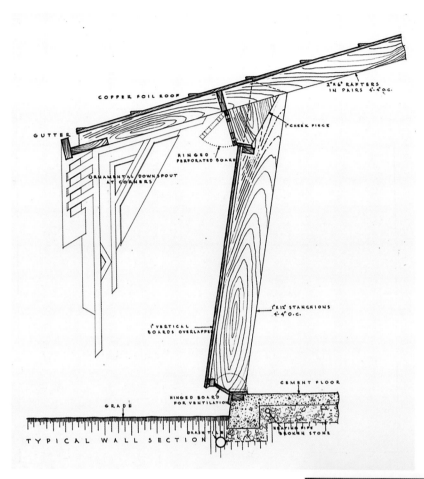

FIG. 55
TYPICAL WALL SECTION
Auldbrass. FLWA 4015.052

FIG. 56
MAIN HOUSE
Auldbrass Wall detail, entry court. Courtesy
Joel Silver, 1989

uous openings through which the horses might escape, alternate boards were to be hinged so they could open, creating a fully ventilated wall. In residential areas where generous, full openings were wanted, Wright designed outward-opening panels of translucent canvas, stretched over a light wood frame like that of a wood stretcher for a large painting. As earlier noted, Stevens questioned the workability of canvas from the beginning,[25] but Wright prevailed, at least at first.

The result of the integrated system of construction Wright devised was a light, permeable, flexible enclosure without exact parallel. The continuous, rambling elements of the composition now assumed a lithe, screen-like pliancy well suited to the warm climate and highly evocative of place. A flat, relatively featureless site would assume heightened definition through architectural intervention. None of this could have been achieved with a conventional plan, or a typical wall section. Thus, it can be argued, Wright achieved his special celebration of place.

Although they were to cause much comment, sloped walls in themselves are far from unknown in the history of architecture. One has only to look at traditional Thai architecture, or Turkish Seljuk tombs, or Pre-Columbian buildings, to gain a sense of their widespread appearance. Wright had already incorporated angled walls in his designs, as in the upper levels of Hollyhock House for Aline Barnsdall (Los Angeles, 1917–21), or the barges and cabins of Lake Tahoe, or in his designs for the Johnson Desert Compound. He would continue to explore their possibilities, as in the Arch Oboler house (Malibu, California, 1940–41, unbuilt) and perhaps most famously in the Solomon R. Guggenheim Museum (1943–59). But the particular instance of Auldbrass is made distinctive by the special system of construction employed. In only one other design, it seems, did he suggest a similar system: the second design for the Martin Pence house (Hilo, Hawaii, 1942), but it remained unbuilt. Ventilation slots can be found in a few examples, as the House on the Mesa (Denver, Colorado, 1931, unbuilt) and the Walker house (Carmel, California, 1949–51), but they were handled in distinctly different ways, being incorporated into systems of glass windows.

Several observers have speculated on the possible iconography of the sloped walls and expressive downspouts. Generally the walls are described as responsive to the oak trees on the property, which incline at a similar angle. Indeed, this similarity is cited on the National Register form listing Auldbrass as an historic monument.[26] According to Stevens's daughter, Wright was fascinated by the amount of weight a slanted trunk could carry.[27] Certainly the angled trees on the property are in sympathy with the similarly angled walls, and their natural slope may have suggested to Wright the direction he took. And what-

ever photographs Stevens may have sent to show Wright his property, images of these leaning trees figure prominently in the books that Stevens had also sent him at the beginning of the commission.[28]

Others liken the copper downspouts at Auldbrass to the Spanish moss hanging from the trees, and again this accords with Stevens's daughter's recollections. In his own description of the property, Wright mentioned the "large moss-hung trees about the whole area . . .".[29] As to the perforated pattern on boards used for ventilating panels and repeated elsewhere in the design, Stevens's daughter describes it as an arrow motif reflecting the Indian ancestry of the land, and recalls, moreover, how these patterns were always referred to as arrows, with the arrowhead usually seen at the lower right and the feathers at the upper left. The numbers of the latter varied according to the different lengths of the windows; the standard number was five, but they could also range up to six and down to one.[30] Later imprinted on stationery, this motif became the symbol of the house (fig. 57).

There is no reason to discount any of these observations. While it seems Wright himself did not record them as his specific intentions, he did recognize and accept such representational conventions, as made clear in his own writings:

the Egyptians 'knew' the Lotus and translated the Lotus to the dignified stone forms of their Architecture: this was the Lotus 'conventionalized!' The Greeks 'knew' and idealized the Acanthus in stone translations. This was the Acanthus conventionalized. Of all Art, whatsoever, perhaps Architecture is the Art best fitted to teach this lesson, for in its practices this problem of 'conventionalizing' nature is worked out at its highest and best.

. . . at this same time it must be organically true to nature when it is really a work of Art. . . . in turning it to stone and fitting it to grace a column capital, the Egyptian artist put it through a rare and difficult process, wherein its natural character was really revealed and intensified in terms of stone, gaining for it an imperishable significance, for the Life principle of the flower is translated to terms of building stone to satisfy the Ideal of a real 'need.' This is Conventionalization, and it is Poetry.[31]

Whatever the imagery, Auldbrass came to epitomize, for Wright, his vision of Southern splendor, of country life that fully celebrated its special location. Like so much of his work, his concept embodies unique qualities of the sort that distinguish his career, qualities intrinsically tied to, and in part derived from, the particular site. And also like so much of his work, the realization of the concept would show him willing to compromise on some aspects, but clear in his determination to preserve the essential qualities of its design.

AULDBRASS
YEMASSEE, SOUTH CAROLINA 29945

FIG. 57
DECORATIVE MOTIF
Auldbrass, from hinged panel, as adapted to
stationery. Courtesy Jessica Loring Stevens

RIGHT
FIG. 58
SMALL BEDROOM, MAIN HOUSE
Auldbrass, showing the Auldbass motif above
the door. Alan Weintraub/Arcaid, 2001

FOLLOWING PAGES
FIG. 59
LIVING ROOM, MAIN HOUSE
Auldbrass, main house, showing decorative
wood panels at perimeter.
Alan Weintraub/Arcaid, 2001

CHAPTER 4

BUILDING AULDBRASS: THE FIRST CAMPAIGN

PREVIOUS PAGES
FIG. 60
MAIN HOUSE
Auldbrass, with kitchen porch on left and
living room on right. Anthony Peres, 2001

OPPOSITE
FIG. 61
MAIN HOUSE
Auldbrass, with pool terrace on left and
lake on right. Paul Rocheleau, 1992

The construction of Auldbrass began in late September, 1940, shortly after the first set of working drawings had been completed.[1] It was an inauspicious time to embark on so ambitious a scheme. The spread of war in Europe had led to shortages of building materials in the United States, partly the result of government controls imposed in response to the impending crisis. These same events had complicated Leigh Stevens's life as well, for increasingly he was called upon to solve crises of production arising as a result, and he found himself with less time than he needed to oversee progress at Auldbrass. Because he patriotically donated much of his time when government contracts were at stake, his finances suffered, leading to further dilemmas with his plantation. Finally, there were problems in positioning the buildings brought about by Wright's lack of familiarity with the site, a surprising oversight in a career so dedicated to excelling in just such efforts.

Other problems would have existed whatever the specific issues of the moment. The angled layout of the plans complicated construction, and these complications were greatly compounded by the inward slope of the walls. The innovative system of wood frame construction that Wright had proposed, and the unusual details of its component parts, were difficult for local builders to understand. Had Wright himself supervised construction, or at least assigned the task to one of his more experienced apprentices, and had Stevens been less prone to interfere during

his sporadic visits, things might have fared better.

The working drawings, for the most part dated between August 7 and August 10, 1940, had been completed under the direction of Jack Howe with the assistance of Curtis Besinger, two senior apprentices who were very experienced indeed.[2] The third of Wright's senior apprentices, Wesley Peters, was assigned to visit the site at the beginning of construction, and Wright was to follow later. Judging from the detailed instructions Stevens conveyed to Wright on how to find the property, it seems clear that it would have been his first actual visit.[3] In the end Wright did not make the trip, but Peters did, arriving in late August, 1940, though only for a short stay. He was replaced in September by a younger and far less experienced apprentice, Peter Berndtson, and it was Berndtson who largely supervised construction during a series of prolonged visits over the months that followed, assisted only occasionally by Peters when the latter's schedule permitted.[4]

Stevens himself apparently selected the contractor for Auldbrass: J. J. McDevitt Company of Charlotte, North Carolina. It was a well-established concern, having been incorporated in 1925 and having begun operation at least as early as 1920. During construction of Auldbrass, the company changed its name to McDevitt & Street Company, and it had been C. P. Street who submitted a formal proposal for construction on September 13, 1940.[5] In that proposal, Street estimated construction costs for the main house to be $17,163; for the guest house, including the connecting passage and car shelter, $28,153; and for the remaining farm buildings, $43,002. Street wrote, "we are very anxious to have this contract," but wisely cautioned,

> It is our belief that there will be many requirements for the type of work indicated which are not specifically set forth in the plans and specifications. Naturally, if the work is awarded on a lump sum basis, the contractor, whoever they may be, will request extra payment for such additional work.[6]

They advised building on a "cost plus fixed fee basis" rather than binding themselves to a fixed estimate. This meant billing directly for labor and materials as they were needed, a more flexible approach when facing challenges of the sort they correctly anticipated. As profit, they proposed a fee of $1,500 for the main house, $2,500 for the guest house, and $3,500 for the farm buildings.[7] To this Stevens agreed, signing a contract dated September 21, 1940, for construction of the farm buildings.[8]

T. F. (Floyd) Haddock, one of McDevitt's longtime employees (he had been with the firm since 1920), was assigned the task of supervising all construction activity at the site, and he remained in this position during the entire

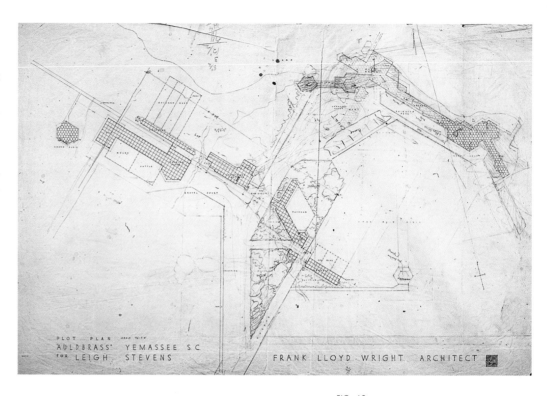

course of McDevitt's construction activity at Auldbrass. As correspondence shows, Haddock became actively involved as intermediary between Wright and Stevens, an unusual situation, considering it is the normal responsibility of the architect to mediate between contractor and client. In other instances, key decisions were often made by Wright and Stevens alone, with no record as to how those decisions might have been transmitted in an orderly manner, or in any manner at all, to Berndtson or Haddock, and confusion often prevailed. Perhaps to atone for his absence at the beginning of construction, Wright sent a lengthy, eight-page memo.[9] In it he pleads for a topographic survey of the property so that he can complete his site plans—clearly no such survey had yet been furnished, beyond the rough sketches and approximate dimensions he had earlier received. Even so, he specified certain approaches to siting. Fences were to be located ten feet back from the roads to allow "for suitable planting," slopes from the house down to the "swamp" were to be landscaped (plans would follow), oak trees on the property were to be left, and gum trees "sorted out" rather than cut.[10]

Questions soon arose regarding materials. Shortages threatened to make substitutions necessary, and even so skilled a manipulator as Stevens, known for his connections to industry and for his ability to solve problems of supply, could not overcome certain barriers. Early on, the question of sheet copper that Wright had wanted for the roofs proved vexing, and well before construction began, as noted, Wright had agreed to substitute copper foil, an inferior material, but one expected to develop the patinated blue-green color he wanted.[11] About its durability Stevens had justifiable doubts. Wright remained steadfast; in bold letters and underlined, he wrote in his eight-page memo of 1940, "important note: no aluminum roofs whatsoever!"[12]

Even more critical to Wright's design was the wood sheathing, to be exposed everywhere, both inside and out. Clear cypress—strong, durable, and indigenous to the area—had by then been selected. It was available, but unduly expensive and in short supply. Beyond its cost, which Stevens agreed to accept, lay problems of size, for the wide boards that Wright wanted could not be found. At first Wright preferred to substitute a cheaper grade of wood rather than abandon the wide boards altogether, as he telegraphed to Stevens in late November, 1940:

Ceilings and partitions should be twelve inch boards but suggest having alternate twelve and six inch boards throughout outer walls putting the six inch boards outside

instead of inside. Interiors then show twelve inch boards everywhere with three inch bands between. . . stanchions and roof timbering must be solid two inch dressed like board walls. If no cypress use redwood. If either aristocrat too expensive use plebeian yellow pine. Honest plebeian no disgrace. Prefer that to shredding everything [using narrower dimensions]. Wide boards necessary to noble effect of building.[13]

Stevens evidently thought otherwise, believing narrower boards of cypress better than wider boards of an inferior grade, whatever Wright's "noble effect." Barely a day after receiving Wright's telegram, Wesley Peters telegraphed Wright, "Stevens from New York orders McDevitt leave present lumber order stand pending his seeing you in Wisconsin. . . . Still pouring concrete here."[14]

By early December, Wright indicated readiness to compromise on the dimensions of the wood: "In view of lumber situation willing to rearrange design using ten inch boards throughout if you desire. Have a way to do this without much harm."[15] Three days later wider boards were found, but in limited quantities, and ways of getting the most out of the twelve-inch boards continued to be discussed for the

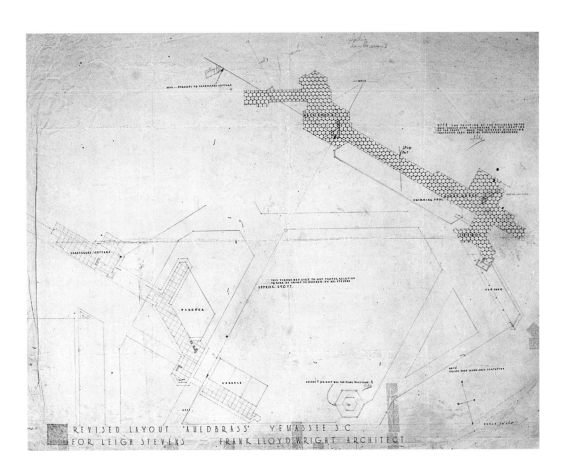

FIG. 63
REVISED PLOT PLAN
Auldbrass. FLWA 4015.017

AERIAL PERSPECTIVE
Auldbrass, showing location of house as built
and its relation to future guest house at upper
right. Eric Lloyd Wright, 2002

next two months.[16] In the end some changes were made, but enough wide boards secured to achieve the effect Wright desired.

Problems also arose early on over a third major component of the design: the canvas panels, or flaps, as Wright termed them, that he wished to use in place of more standard glass doors. They were to be the primary means by which each room opened out to adjoining terraces and exterior views, and Stevens doubted that anything so lightweight and impermanent could actually work.[17] Wright remained steadfast, sending samples of the canvas he had selected in mid-December.[18] Stevens tentatively agreed, yet his doubts remained.

While debate over the canvas flaps continued, concrete slabs were being poured for the farm buildings, yet with incomplete details regarding the framing of the buildings to be erected upon them. Haddock was fearful of unknown complexities that might emerge during later phases of building and asked for more detailed plans.[19] Construction continued in any case, and by mid-February 1941, photographs of completed sections were sent to Wright so that he might judge the appearance of the copper foil roofing, which he liked. But the framing of roofs that were to link the separate building elements—by then a critical need—remained a puzzle until early March, when additional drawings were sent.[20]

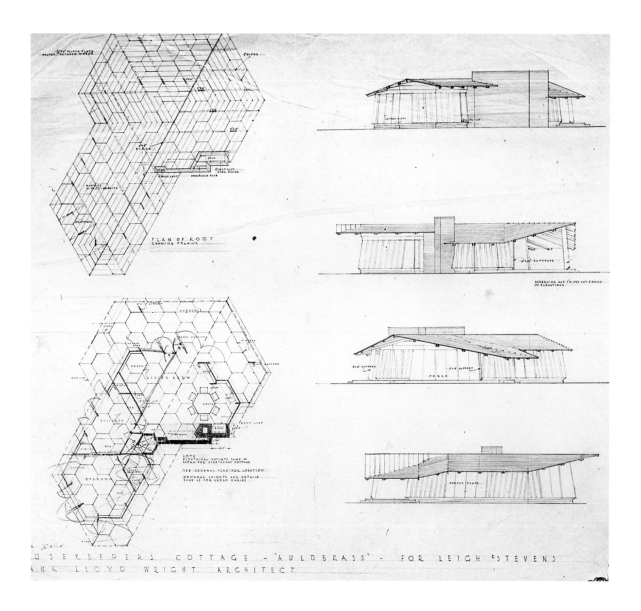

HOUSEKEEPERS COTTAGE — "AULDBRASS" — FOR LEIGH STEVENS
ANK LLOYD WRIGHT ARCHITECT

FIG. 65
**PLANS AND ELEVATIONS
OF HOUSEKEEPER'S COTTAGE**
Auldbrass. FLWA 4026.001

Part of the problem relating to the framing of the interconnected roofs related to their height, for Wright was determined to maintain a low proportion, and an even line, whatever the consequences. It became apparent that the dramatic, low-slung, triangular trusses he wanted for the machinery shed, if held to this level, would leave insufficient headroom. He claimed to have solved the problem by adjusting floor levels "without destroying domestic proportions of our scheme"[21]. In the end he indeed maintained the "domestic proportions" effected by the low, continuous roofs, but the machinery never really fit, and instead, in later years, would remain parked outside.[22]

During the spring of 1941 more problems arose. Stevens became increasingly frustrated in his attempts to communicate with Wright and to secure better supervision of his project. There was no telephone then at Taliesin West, and Wright repeatedly missed appointments to be waiting for Stevens's call by the closest available telephones at either the Arizona Biltmore in Scottsdale, or the somewhat closer Kiami Lodge. In one telegram Stevens harangues Wright for missing yet another appointment and continues, ". . . please have Wes Yemassee May seventh for rest of week . . . we do not know about glass doors, dog kennel roof, room doors, caretakers [doors] which will not open, shelving horse and cow stable details and a host of minor construction details . . .".[23] Haddock, busy pouring concrete, building furniture and bull sheds, admitted to Wes Peters, "I don't know how to cut my rafter ends . . . dry cypress a joke . . . water is running out of it and it's plenty crooked."[24]

Stevens's reference to "glass doors" is the first indication that he had prevailed, and that glass was being substituted for canvas. Undated pencil sketches over elevation drawings record the alteration: angled muntins and mullions were to be added to the individual doors as they were changed from a single panel of stretched canvas to a more heavily framed panel with divided panes.[25] By the summer of 1941 the transformation seems to have been completed, with canvas flaps eliminated from both the main house and the farm buildings. Only the staff cabins, it seems, were actually built with canvas flaps, and they were still in place when Stevens's daughter sold the property in 1979.[26] If there were any problems with these few examples, they were evidently not recorded.

With the almost total elimination of the canvas flaps and the substitution of glass doors, the question of screens came into focus. Their need was unquestioned, but how to provide them for sloping floor-to-ceiling doors that opened outward (and necessarily upward) remained unanswered. Clearly Wright sought a solution that would not compromise the sense of continuous, permeable openness. One possibility, it seems, involved the adaptation of retractable shades such as manufactured by the Aeroshade Company, with whom Wright's office communicated regarding the job. These could be rolled down from the top like a window shade, but would run in light metal tracks, which could be angled so they were parallel to the sloping doors. The hardware Wright needed, however, was not stocked, and materials needed to fabricate his custom design were unavailable.[27] Ultimately, wood-framed, sliding screen doors were installed in the main house, placed inside and sloped so they were parallel to the doors, but their heavy frames and cumbersome tracks detracted from the otherwise lithe appearance of the permeable walls.

Fewer questions arose regarding furniture for the caretaker's house, the first residential unit of the complex to reach completion. Characteristically, Wright had conceived the pieces as integral components of his design; they were to be of the same cypress as the building itself, and the supporting pedestals of the various tables, beds, and chairs were to be angled just as the walls.[28] There, at least, design coherence was maintained, and the problem of insect screening was solved by Wright's addition of a large porch to be placed along the side of the building facing the main house. It was constructed with a frame of metal pipe, like a trellis, with its top as well as sides infilled by screen.

During the summer of 1941, as the caretaker's house

FIG. 66
PLAN, SECTIONS AND ELEVATIONS OF BATH HOUSE
Auldbrass. FLWA 4030.0056

FOLLOWING PAGES
FIG. 67
FARM BUILDINGS
Auldbrass, with caretaker's house at center and rebuilt wing at right. Anthony Peres, 2001

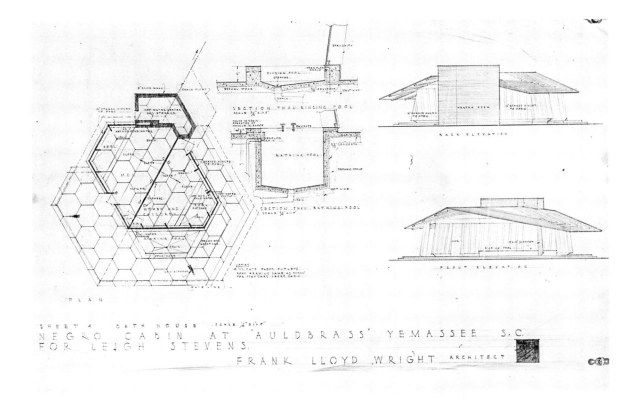

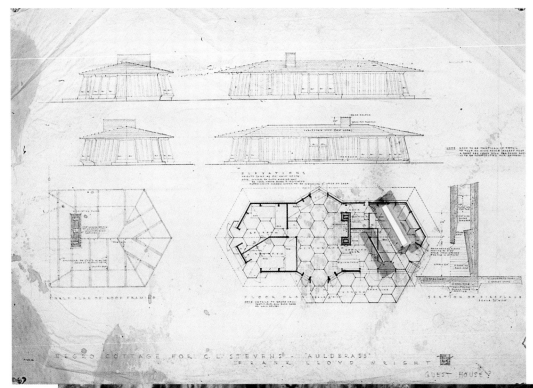

ABOVE
FIG. 70
INTERIOR
Auldbrass, staff cabin, 1941. *Charleston News & Courier;* from the collections of the South Carolina Historical Society

RIGHT
FIG. 71
VIEW TOWARD INTERIOR
Auldbrass staff cabin, as restored. Alan Weintraub/Arcaid, 2001

FIG. 72
AULDBRASS
View to grain and hay barn (at left), cattle and mule stalls (right foreground), chicken sheds beyond (far right; 1941). Auldbrass. *Charleston News & Courier*; from the collections of the South Carolina Historical Society

and adjacent farm buildings neared completion, Wright made major changes to the plans of the remaining components of the plantation, in large part, it seems, to correct his imperfect knowledge of the site. Stevens was anxious to begin construction on the main house, but Wright had retrieved the working drawings in order to make these changes. Unknowing of the need for any changes, or what the changes might be, Stevens was nevertheless willing to trust his architect's judgment as long as the drawings were promptly returned.[29]

Penciled notations in Wright's hand, made over an earlier plot plan, reveal his intentions (fig. 62). The positions of the main house and guest house were to be reversed, with the main house brought closer to the center of the overall composition and the guest house, together with its covered parking, moved further away. This led to a complete reversal, or flipping, of the plans of the two buildings. The aviary is retitled tea pavilion, but its position left unchanged; clearly its role within the composition remained important whatever its function. Suggesting

greater attention to questions of landscape, dwarf azaleas are now indicated within the crisply delineated triangle adjacent to the main gateway through the linear farm buildings—an early specification of cultivated plantings, in this instance reinforcing the geometry of the layout.

A more developed sketch of this layout, apparently done in haste but not in Wright's hand, shows the aviary/tea house enlarged and re-titled "housekeeper."[30] Next came a more formally drafted plan labeled "Revised Layout," again with notations in Wright's hand. He asks, "Aviary? (or what was the final decision?)"[31] Other notes suggest uncertainty as to important topographical features. For example, the dimension between the farm buildings and house is shown as 290 feet, with the modifying statement, "This figure may vary to get proper relation to bank of swamp as desired by Mr. Stevens." The axis of the house is described as parallel to that of the caretaker's cottage, but Wright noted, "the position of the building on the axis should vary according to the location of the trees. Only the general direction indicated here need be pre-

LEFT
FIG. 73
STABLES (ORIGINALLY FOR MARSH TACKIES)
Auldbrass. Courtesy Joel Silver

BELOW
FIG. 74
STABLES (ORIGINALLY FOR CATTLE AND MULES)
Auldbrass. Paul Rocheleau, 2003

cisely observed." Finally, "drives here shown only tenta-
tive." The date of the drawing is obscured, but above it, in
Wright's hand, "void—see new plan."

The "new plan," presumably, is the still more formally
drafted but otherwise identical arrangement, also titled
"Revised Layout . . .", on which the handwritten notes
quoted above have been carefully transcribed (fig. 63).[32]
No date is visible, but Wright has again added notes for
further revisions. Beyond the detached kitchen of the main
house, and extending its linear axis, he has indicated an
approximate location of a "cottage for house servants."
On the slope between the house and now more distant line
of the "swamp," he has asked, "planting down the
swamp?" Nearer the house, between the kitchen and the
house servants' cottage, he noted "garden" and "walls?",
the latter clearly indicating the low garden walls that would
be developed in later plans.

Other than these diagrammatic plans, it seems no
drawings showing the changed configuration of the house

and guest house were prepared, leaving Stevens with little indication as to the appearance that might result.
Had a new aerial perspective been drawn, it would no
doubt have resembled the rendering by Eric Lloyd
Wright, done in the style of the 1940 perspective to fill
this gap (fig. 64).

A housekeeper's cottage had been designed soon
after construction began in the fall of 1940 (fig. 65), but
like the staff cabins its exact location was left unspecified.
It was one of several elements designed for Auldbrass that
seemed to have no fixed place. A bath house for the staff,
resembling one of the staff cabins, but modified with the
addition of a bathing and rinsing pools, had been
designed in August, 1940 (fig. 66); it, too, was unlocated. A drawing dated March 1941, shows a larger
staff cottage, a symmetrical building that in form recalls
the Lake Tahoe barges, and that Wright thought might
also serve as a guest house, but nothing indicates further
development (fig. 68). Among these various unbuilt and

even unlocated components—and more were to follow—the housekeeper's cottage alone would claim more urgent attention.

Late in July 1941, more anxious than ever to begin its construction, Stevens telegraphed impatiently for his plans of the main house.[33] Wright replied, "Redrawn plans. . . scheme reversed . . . sent Yemassee. Good luck."[34] Clearly these are the surviving set of working drawings that Wright's office had produced by reconfiguring the August 1940, set. As made clear through an examination of these drawings, the lettered notes of the earlier working drawings were first erased, then reverse prints made by running the tracings through the duplicating machine with the drafted surface facing down rather than up to obtain the reversed image. The new prints—made on translucent paper, so they, in turn, could be readily duplicated—were then re-lettered and redated July 1941. Although somewhat painstaking, this process yielded a new set of working drawings with greater speed than would have been the case if the full set were redrawn. Over the months that followed, these drawings were themselves revised (a workable process with eradicating fluid used to erase the printed lines), and new drawings were made to supplement the set. Revised working drawings for the guest house were produced in a similar manner to those of the main house and sent soon after.[35]

Still missing was a complete layout showing the locations of all the buildings on the plantation. Soon after receiving the newly produced working drawings, Stevens protested, "you sent no reverse plot plan so we cannot lay out main house . . .".[36] Eugene Masselink sent a drawing the next day, asking that it be returned so he could make copies.[37] Perhaps he had felt it wiser to send it at once rather than incur delay by having a print made in Phoenix. Exactly which drawing Masselink sent is uncertain. Later correspondence reflects much debate over who might have the original of the revised plot plan; other plans were drawn, and at least one was lost. But in spite of this confusion the revised plot plan was immediately implemented, and the plan of the main house accordingly reversed.

Nothing documents the precise reason why Wright reversed his layout. The views from the main house in either location would have been approximately the same—if anything, more expansive in the first. An apparent need to position previously unsited elements—in particular, the housekeeper's cottage—may partly account for the adjustment. What seems most likely to have provoked the change, however, was insufficient knowledge of the site, as already mentioned. Earlier drawings show the line of the adjacent bank inaccurately, with the house and guest house making connections to it in a manner that would have been quite impossible. This would have become apparent to both Wesley Peters and Peter Berndtson, even without Wright's presence. As reversed, the exterior profiles of each building related more effectively to the actual line of the bank, which curved differently and at a greater distance from the intended location of the buildings than shown in the first design drawings. And the bank was not steep, although Wright had imaginatively portrayed it as such in early perspectives.

Still vexing is the question of how Wright, the master of siting and an acknowledged genius in perceiving specific qualities of topography, could have missed these features. According to Jessica Stevens Loring, Wright and her father walked the site together, selecting the location for the house at the outset of the commission, before any drawings had been completed.[38] Yet this may not have been the case. Stevens's daughter did not visit the site in these years; indeed, her first visit was not until the early 1950s. She relied instead on her father's descriptions of these events. He, in turn, may have forgotten, or may have wished to add to the mythology of its design. As the correspondence makes clear, Wright repeatedly scheduled visits, then cancelled his plans. His only documented visit to the site came later, in May 1942, well after most of the construction had been completed.[39] This would accord with Stevens's comment to his third wife, that Wright only visited the site once.[40] No wonder, then, that Wright so urgently requested accurate topographical surveys, and despaired when they were not forthcoming. No wonder that he chose to revise the plans on his own when discrepancies were discovered.

On August 21, 1941, with the revised plans in place and while the farm buildings were still being completed, Stevens authorized McDevitt to begin construction on the main house.[41] Details continued to plague the builders—getting the gutters of the farm buildings to fit along an even horizontal line and clear the doors was particularly vexing.[42] Haddock wrote that one of the doors "will hit gutters if built as detailed," while Wright's office continued to insist that the "gutter line must remain the same throughout."[43] Frustrated by Wright's distance from the site, Stevens wrote,

Please do not ask me to go through another winter with you in Arizona waiting for minor details. If Berndtson had been competent, I would have had my house finished by now with a savings of several thousand dollars. I would like to have all the details settled with you so I can go through with it.[44]

Given his professional ties to the building industry, it is hardly surprising that Stevens took an increasingly active role in supervising construction himself, making changes as he saw fit. Some he communicated to Wright, and apparently awaited Wright's approval.[45] Others he made on his own. T. F. Haddock wrote to Wesley Peters,

Looks like another year in these here swamps. Bro. Stevens is having more fun changing and altering his house. . . . Peter [Berndtson] tried to place [the plumbing fixtures in the saddle room] so as to give more room, and got cussed out for his pain. Well you can tell him Bro. Stevens is giving him his again for putting them where Stevens himself marked them to go. . . . This is all the latest scandal so will close. . . .".[46]

Not long after, Haddock wrote again, "starting myself another year . . . Bro. Stevens is still in full stride of changing of things each time he stops talking long enough to think."[47]

During the fall of 1941, a sense of emergency caused by the escalating war in Europe added pressures. Urgent requests were made to Wright's office for details so that such critical items as plumbing fixtures and hardware could be ordered for the main house while some stocks were still available.[48] Estimates for furniture for the main house were requested from cabinet makers, again with the realization that wood, too, was in short supply.[49] Much remained to be resolved; Stevens arranged a telephone interview with Wright for December 7, 1941.[50] The bombing of Pearl Harbor that day precipitated America's immediate entry into World War II, and the call was forgotten, but work on Auldbrass continued.

ABOVE
FIG. 79
STAFF CABIN
Auldbrass, with built-in bed, 1941.
Charleston News & Courier; courtesy South Carolina
Historical Society

LEFT
FIG. 78
CARETAKER'S HOUSE
Auldbrass. Courtesy South Carolina Historical
Society.

Ongoing construction at Auldbrass, easily visible from the road, excited local curiosity. *The Charleston News and Courier* requested permission to publish a story on the project; apparently it was Wright who gave permission rather than Stevens.[51] Photographs for the story, taken during the fall of 1941, show the farm buildings as nearly complete and the main house in its beginning stages.[52] The angled siding and low, gently gabled roofs linking separate elements seem very much a part of their setting (figs. 72, 75). Spanish moss frames the views in a manner that would surely have appealed to Wright, and the lines of the copper foil roofs are still pristine (fig. 69, 78, 81). Interior views of one of the two staff cabins that had been built show even the furniture completed, including built-in sofas and a dining table with angled, hexagonal stools (fig. 70). In the narrow corridor of the caretaker's house, another view shows an opened ventilating panel at the base of the wall, providing an unexpected vista (fig. 82). Elsewhere, other buildings appear less finished, and all that can be seen of the main house is the shape of its floor slab, outlined by formwork with radiant heating coils in place, but the concrete as yet unpoured (fig. 77).

In other photographs, the young women being used as models seem oddly positioned, as if to exaggerate the buildings' peculiar features for an unknowing public (fig. 79). This proved intentional. The newspaper story, which ran on December 21, 1941, ridiculed the design as an "angled crazy house."[53] Infuriated, Stevens gave orders that no further photography was to be allowed, and he closed the site to all visitors. The story was picked up by the *Charlotte Sunday Observer*, which ran a full-page spread (with a selection of the earlier pictures) on January 4, 1942, under the headline, "The 'Crazy Plantation' Near Yemassee, S.C., Has Native Folk A-Talking—and Swooning!" (fig. 80).[55] The next day Stevens wrote to Wright, "I am badly in need of a gate design as I am being pestered by the visitors."[56] The design was a bit long in coming (the drawing is dated July 2, 1943), but firmly responsive to the grammar of the project, with angled boards enclosing a triangular entrance court (fig. 84). The informal axis of the entrance driveway, which met the road at an angle of sixty degrees, sustained the elegant quality of informal ease.

In addition to a gate, Stevens also wrote in January of 1942 that he was "badly in need of the brooder house design."[57] Wright's hexagonal plan that followed (undated) recalls the diagrammatic poultry enclosures of the ideal monastery plan in the Chapter library at St. Gall, Switzerland (this historic drawing is dated ca. 820).[58] On his drawing (fig. 86) Wright inscribed, "I don't remember too clearly what you exactly wanted—but know well this [will] do for the chickens," a clear reference to his own pride in raising poultry at Taliesin.

Charlotte Sunday Observer

FINANCIAL
CLASSIFIED
BUILDERS

Leads All North Carolina And South Carolina Newspapers In News And Features

FOUNDED 1869   CHARLOTTE, N. C., SUNDAY MORNING, JANUARY 4, 1942   PRICE: 5c DAILY—10c SUNDAY

The 'Crazy Plantation' Near Yemassee, S. C. Has Native Folk A-talking--And Swooning!

RIGHT ANGLES AND VERTICLES ARE RULED OUT

Rich Man Wanted Something Different, and He's Getting It!

CEDAR BUNKS FOR DOGS

Copper Roof Tops Look Like Milady's Latest Hat; No Windows, No Nails.

BY SAM A. COTHRAN.

THERE'S NOTHING CROSS-EYED HERE--IT'S 'CRAZY PLANTATION'

HERE are seven scenes of the Auld Brass plantation, near Yemassee, S. C., in the low country—a plantation that's different, no right angles and no verticles, the roofs go up and down, the walls slant in all directions; it's so unusual the natives are calling it the "crazy house."

Picture No. 1—The pretty misses, tired after a tour of the place, sit down and gaze into the nature-infested marshlands which surround the plantation. The building is a tenant house at the entrance to the plantation—and the visitor's first shock. The spaces to the right are the doors. Since there are no windows in any of the buildings, the doors will be of glass and none of them will be square or rectangular. The

Picture No. 2—Miss Edith Mixon of Yemassee and Miss Ethel Margaret Gatch, also of Yemassee (left), are busy viewing some of the odd fixtures in the tap room for tenants. Mrs. M. O. Lane, Jr., is shown at right inspecting the fireplace.

Picture No. 3—Miss Gatch, nearly cross-eyed from the various views, is shown leaning against one of the slanting walls of a bedroom in one of the tenant houses. The bed, incidentally, is six-sided.

Picture No. 4—Miss Edith Mixon, contrary to the pictorial evidence, is standing upright. The leaning walls of the stable for Financier C. Leigh Stevens'

of the many intricate panel openings of one of the buildings which will serve as a combination stable and living space for tenants. The hallway shown in the photo as closely as anything comparable, resembles a pullman car arrangement, with rooms on one side and closets on the other.

Picture No. 6—It's not surprising when the visitors discover that this long line of stalls was built for the fine hunting dogs which will be on the plantation. The bunks, by the way, are of the finest cedar, and the dogs will be taught to sleep in them.

Picture No.7—It's a relief when the young women find something commonplace like a farm tractor which brings them back to earth.

U. S. RUSSIAN PLANES TO HIT JAPS IN SPRING

Orientologist Says They Will Fly From Vladivostok.

WINTER HELPS JAPAN

Tokyo Government Picked Right Time Of Year to Launch Its Campaign.

BY J. W. SNYDER.
(Copyright, 1941, Overseas News Agency, Inc.)

FIG. 80
CHARLOTTE SUNDAY OBSERVER
Section Four, page one, January 4, 1942

OPPOSITE
FIG. 81
COOK SHED
Auldbrass, main gateway at left.
Courtesy South Carolina Historical Society.

Stevens built neither the gate nor the brooder house, nor did he build an oddly out-of-character small cabin, square in shape with vertical walls, its design dated June 12, 1942 (fig. 87). Like the bath house and large staff cottage, it remained an undeveloped, undiscussed fragment. The only real clue as to its odd design was Stevens's early statement that cabins for farm workers tended to be square in plan; Wright seems to have sketched such a plan as a kind of note, together with the notation "Aeroshade 001" (a reference to the window treatment he was considering in late 1941) on the preliminary site plan of 1939.

While designs for these disparate elements accumulated during 1942, work continued on the main house. In early January, Stevens had reported "the contractors have finished at last . . .",[59] but he could only have meant its rough enclosure, for correspondence shows the McDevitt Company actively involved with the project through September of that year, and McDevitt later claimed that

work continued until December 28, 1942.[60] Indeed, Stevens did not formally accept the work as completed until December 31, 1942.[61] Stevens's claim of early January, 1942, does suggest, however, that fewer problems had been encountered in framing the main house than in building the farm buildings, and that it had been possible to construct it more quickly, as Wright had no doubt promised. Given the relative simplicity of Wright's system—boards screwed to stanchions or to each other, with no other framing members, no insulation, a simple system of wiring—this seems reasonable, at least once the workers had come to understand the system as a result of first building the farm buildings.

During 1942, as work on the main house neared completion, attention shifted to smaller details. Screening was to be added to the breezeway linking the house to its detached kitchen; Wright at first wavered as to how, then in May approved an elaborate and perhaps unworkable system, in

ABOVE
FIG. 82

CORRIDOR

Auldbrass, caretaker's house,1941.
Charleston News & Courier; from the collections
of the South Carolina Historical Society

RIGHT
FIG. 83

LIVING ROOM

Auldbrass, caretaker's house, showing
new bookcases and passage to bedrooms at left. Alan Weintraub/Arcaid, 2001

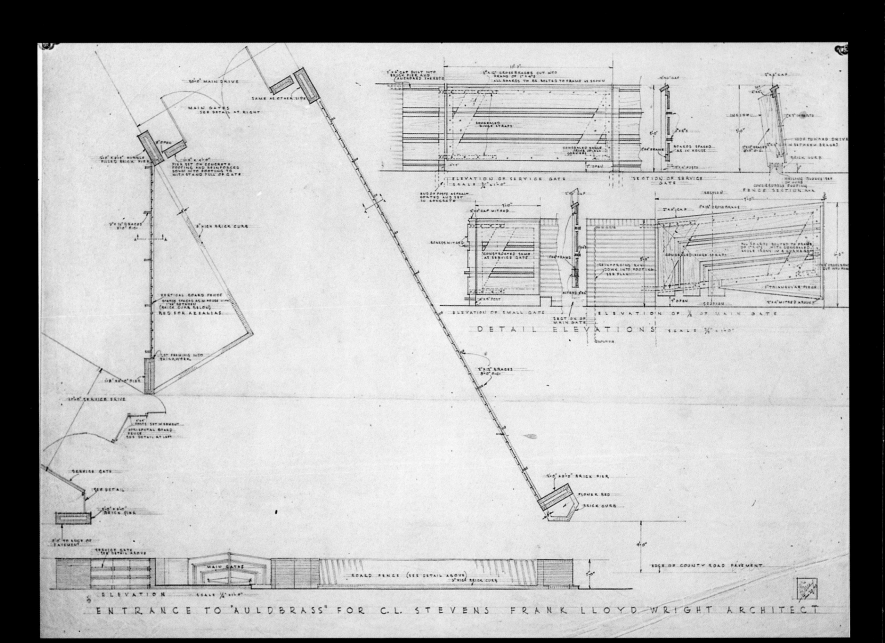

ENTRANCE TO "AULDBRASS" FOR C.L. STEVENS   FRANK LLOYD WRIGHT ARCHITECT

which the screen was to be treated like fabric, hung from the outer edge of the roof overhangs and gathered in at the base.[62] This scheme was abandoned, and no further attempt to screen the breezeway was made for several years. Wright and Stevens debated the best means to finish the cypress where exposed to the elements. To bolster the logic of his solution, Wright enlisted the help of George Affleck, for whom he had recently designed a house in Bloomfield Hills, Michigan (1940). Affleck was asked to tell Stevens how well his Michigan house looked, and to advise him that the finish Wright specified would yield the same result at Auldbrass. Affleck dutifully wrote, "Our house now looks better than it did a year ago as the wood sort of mellows with age."[63] Wright's choice of clear, liquid creosote was then applied, producing the rich, honey-toned color desired.[64]

Still other questions arose dealing with final details. The doors and windows, as well as the furniture, for the main house were to be more finely crafted than had been built by the carpenters elsewhere on the project, requiring the services of a millworker. The contract was awarded to a man Wright had worked with on earlier projects, including the Affleck house: John T. Lyman, of Montclair, New Jersey. Yet even Lyman had questions regarding what he considered to be a very odd series of shapes. He could not have been overly assured by Wesley Peter's initial response to questions regarding the complicated angles: "you will note that in regard to the windows it is pretty difficult to give the exact angle of the meeting stile cut due to the fact that windows are sloping inwards and any slight variation causes considerable trouble."[65] Lyman also questioned a projecting edge on a dining table: "I would think this would be mightily uncomfortable for the person's arms who have to eat at this table. Would it not be better to keep this flush with the top?"[66] Wright wanted no changes whatsoever—any alterations would complicate relationships to other units, and he further argued that the raised edge was slight "and will cause little or no trouble."[67] Stevens occasionally suggested ideas of his own for the interiors of the house. He selected some pieces made by Modernage Furniture that he felt appropriate to use, and had pictures sent to Wright. While these pictures seem to have disappeared, advertisements at the time showing Modernage furniture suggest what Stevens might have had in mind: respectable, rather plain, boxy, and generically modern pieces, but hardly distinctive in the way Wright's were intended. Wright replied, "The Modernage sends cuts of some rather nightmarish furniture which I hope is only one of your bad dreams."[68] No more was heard of this proposal.

Wright, meanwhile, was busily selecting fabric and carpets at Marshall Field & Company in Chicago.[69] They prepared estimates for draperies, cushions, and bedspreads, and for an elaborate carpet to be made of differently col-

ored hexagonal segments pieced together like a giant quilt.[70] Salesmen questioned the triangular outline at the foot of the bedspreads, unaware (understandably) that the beds had such angles.[71] The estimated cost for twenty pairs of draperies—unlined, untrimmed, unpleated Samona cloth in chartreuse, yellow, and ivory—came to $427.83.[72] Estimates for the carpet were being prepared in January 1943, but by then their stocks were rapidly diminishing. Stevens failed to open an account, or to put a reserve on their remaining supplies, and they were presumably sold to another buyer, rendering the need for an estimate moot.[73]

As Wright's attention to detail shows, he remained closely involved with the building of Auldbrass whatever his other obligations, and he came to regard Stevens as one of his most important clients. This became apparent early in 1943 when he included Stevens's name in a long list of acquaintances he thought politically influential, some clients and some not, but all prominent. He asked each to sign a "citizens' petition" on his behalf, an outgrowth of his belief that work at Taliesin was itself important to the war effort. Nineteen of his apprentices had been drafted into military service, and three others detained as conscientous objectors.[74] Earlier he had claimed, "Taliesin is a training field for young builders. The work here is of great importance, so we all believe, to the country that is fighting . . .".[75] Now he circulated his petition, prefacing his request for support with the words, "Feeling that now is a good time for an able bodied architect like myself who would be in the way on the firing line to get busy for our country I choose my own weapons and fight for Democracy and a true capitalist system my way."[76] The petition itself, which Stevens signed, reflects much of Wright's personal idealism at the time:

> We, the undersigned, respectfully ask that the Administration of our Government authorize Frank Lloyd Wright to continue the search for Democratic FORM as the basis for a true capitalist society now known as Broadacre City. We believe that work should immediately be declared a worthy national objective and the necessary ways and means freely granted him to make such plans, models and drawings as will enable our citizens and other peoples to comprehend the basic ideas the plans, models and drawings represent and which, without political bias or influences will be invaluable to our people when peace is being considered.[77]

By then, Stevens was encountering severe difficulties of his own. Auldbrass had cost far more than originally projected, yet was still unfinished. And just when more funds were needed to pay debts incurred by construction, less was coming in. For as noted,

FIG. 84
PLAN, ELEVATION, AND DETAILS
Entrance to Auldbrass. FLWA 4025.002

FOLLOWING PAGES
FIG. 85
MAIN GATEWAY
Auldbrass, through farm buildings.
Anthony Peres, 2001

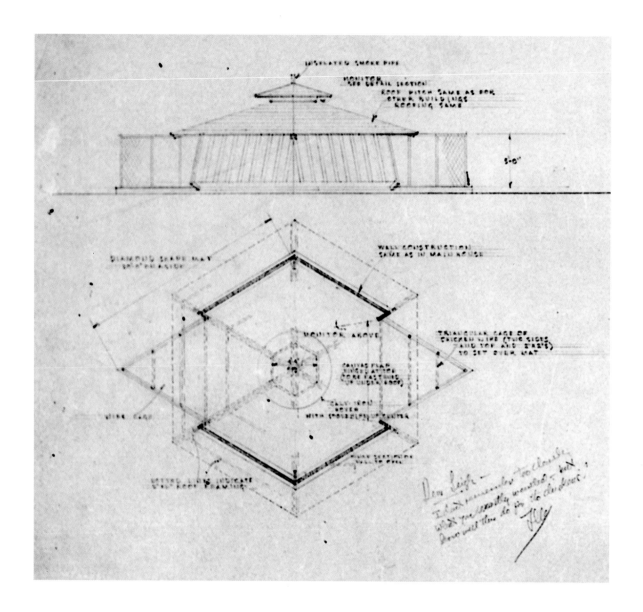

rather than charging consulting fees to which he would be entitled, he reportedly volunteered his services during the war, describing himself as "a dollar-a-year man," and drawing instead on his dwindling financial reserves.[78] And the record of his work during the war is impressive. He served as a special adviser to Donald M. Nelson, Chairman of the War Production Board; to General Robert W. Johnson, of the Smaller War Plants Corporation; and was involved in the highly secretive Manhattan project, which was developing the atomic bomb.[79] Understandably he was absent from Auldbrass for long periods, and not easily reachable.

Wright was among those who grew concerned by Stevens's seeming disappearance during the early 1940s. After trying without success to contact Stevens, he wrote, "You aren't sick or something are you? I am anxious."[80] With less tact, others, wanting money, pursued him more openly. Lyman, finishing the cabinetwork, wrote, "Poor Stevens. His job is being sorely neglected. . . . It is a hell of a time for a millionaire to decide to finish a house anyway. Besides he pays his bills as slow as Wesley Peters and is just as elusive."[81] Later Lyman conferred with Wright as to where Stevens might be found, and to another Wright client he wrote that Stevens remained in hiding, adding, "Such colossal nerve in a man I have never seen."[82] Ever persistent, Lyman next tracked Stevens to Washington, where he confronted him in the Mayflower Hotel. He demanded payment, but was told that no money was available.[83] Lyman began receiving his money in January, 1945, but in small increments, suggesting that Stevens's financial situation remained tight.[84]

McDevitt & Street pursued Stevens another way. On March 13, 1943, they initiated legal proceedings, filing a lien against the property in an effort to recover $38,432.20 that they claimed Stevens still owed them.[85] According to court records, the work had been completed on December 28, 1942, at a cost of $84,537.66. Stevens had paid only $46,105.46. He failed to appear at the ensuing hearing, and on May 24, 1943, McDevitt filed for foreclosure on the property, petitioning that Auldbrass be sold "by the Clerk of the Court for Beaufort County at the Courthouse door at Beaufort during the legal hours of sale on the 1st Monday in June, 1944 . . .".[86] Before that date, on September 22, 1943, some four months after McDevitt had filed for foreclosure, Stevens paid an additional $10,000, yet this did not deter McDevitt in pressing his case, and in December, 1943, his company renewed their petition that Auldbrass be sold.[87]

Stevens again failed to appear at a hearing on April 24, 1944, and a court referee recommended that McDevitt's claim be recognized and the property indeed be sold.[88] Before that happened, McDevitt and Stevens settled their differences out of court, and the case was formally dismissed on December 19, 1944.[89] Records fail to show how the settlement was reached, but ownership of Auldbrass was at least secured again. How ironic it is that Stevens, who worked assiduously to protect his property from seizure in any divorce, should so nearly lose it by a more routine procedure.

By the time of these various settlements, work had long since stopped at Auldbrass, for there is no evidence of any construction after December 1942.[90] Interiors were left unfinished, plumbing fixtures and other components were missing, Stevens was no longer there. To those who passed by, it must have seemed an abandoned folly.

RIGHT
FIG. 87
PLANS, ELEVATIONS, AND DETAILS
Auldbrass, small cabin and fence. FLWA 4029.003

FOLLOWING PAGES
FIG. 88
THE LAKE
Auldbrass, from main house, showing detail of copper roof pendant. Paul Rocheleau, 1992

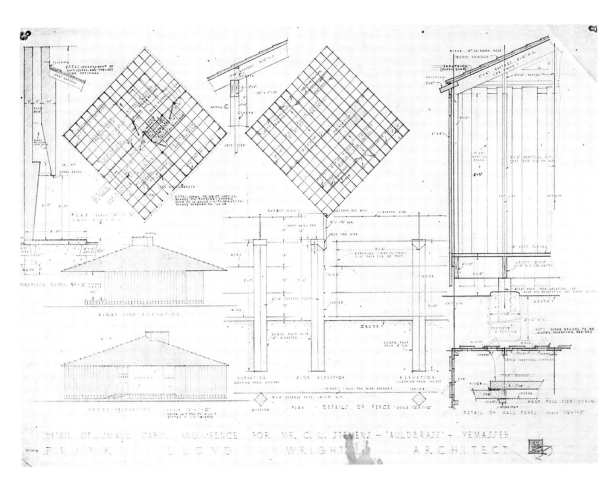

The next building campaigns at Auldbrass encompassed a period of sixteen years, from 1946 to 1962. Following his first divorce in 1941, Stevens married for a second time in 1942. He was to divorce and remarry twice more during this period. With each wife, designs were altered to reflect new wishes, so the project never seemed to be completed.[1] Wright accepted this situation. "Places are never finished as long as a new and worthwhile idea comes up," he explained to Stevens's third wife early in her ascendancy. "Your place, like this one [Taliesin], can suggest a new idea overnight."[2]

About his second wife Stevens's family remembers little, except that her first name was Ann and she came from Savannah.[3] Typically his wives remained in the shadow of his active career. Ann, it seems, had little interest in Auldbrass, although Stevens tried to involve her in its completion.

Following the war, Stevens quickly reestablished his consulting business. He worked with the government to restructure the textile industry in the South and served as advisor to the United Nations on matters related to food and agriculture. Other clients included both the U.S. Department of State and the Ford Foundation. Nehru, Pope Pius XII, Chiang Kai-Shek and Syngman Rhee all sought his advice at one time or another.[4] Funds were soon available to resume work at Auldbrass, but the very work that produced those funds required extensive travel, and supervision became even more difficult than in earlier years. Frequently away for long periods of time, he

would leave with little or no notice. Departing abruptly on the night of his third marriage, he explained to his wife of a few hours, "Often my plans are top-secret. . . . It's a question of making big money. I need that kind of money to finish Auldbrass as it should be finished."[5] Yet making such money also instigated periods of neglect, for his workers hesitated to proceed without his personal directions.[6]

Stevens had reached his decision to resume construction by April 1946, hopeful that Auldbrass might soon be ready for him to occupy. As he wrote to Frank Lloyd Wright, "I've decided to follow your advice and finish Auld Brass."[7] They met at Taliesin West soon after; within a matter of days Stevens sent Wright a retainer and asked for a drawing of yet another component he had evidently sketched during their discussions: a large, very simple staff cabin, this time with three bedrooms and bath (but still no heat).[8] An odd, undated drawing may reflect Wright's efforts to oblige Stevens's request (fig. 90). Crudely drafted, it appears to be the work of a junior apprentice. Conventionally rectangular with flat roofs and vertical walls, it bears no resemblance to the rest of Auldbrass, and its unpleasant, but efficient, layout indeed suggests a client's solution. The drawings are rudely crossed out, perhaps by Wright himself, and no other record of this element can be found, nor any of the U-shaped farm building shown in plan on the right side of the sheet.

Whatever the situation regarding this soon abandoned proposal, Stevens reacted favorably to renewed ties with his architect. "Now that I've decided to go ahead I find myself most dependent on you," he wrote. "I keep remembering your remark about not being fair to your design. . . . But anyhow it's a good feeling to be at it again. . . . I do hope nothing now gets in the way."[9] Wright's reply: "It is nice to know that effort of ours is not to be wasted."[10]

That fall Stevens moved into Auldbrass "on a camping-out basis."[11] His daughter later used the same words to describe how Stevens first lived there: "he camped out. . .".[12] As she knew from her later visit to the site, it was not in the main house (then still far from habitable), but instead in the more nearly complete caretaker's house that Stevens arranged his temporary quarters.

Wright worked to change this situation. His first drawings, dated November and December, 1946, resumed where his last had stopped before the war. One deals with the interiors of the main house; proposals for curtains, bedspreads, and pillows are worked out in greater detail, but their colors—yellows, ivories, and greens—remain unchanged. Also unchanged is the elaborately pieced carpet that he had earlier specified (fig. 91). A special lounge chair was designed for the living room, to be followed by other pieces for Mrs. Stevens's bedroom.[13]

New working drawings were prepared for the guest house, adding more guest rooms (a total of eleven are

FIG. 90
PLAN AND ELEVATION OF STAFF CABIN AND FARM BUILDING
Auldbrass. FLWA 4028.009

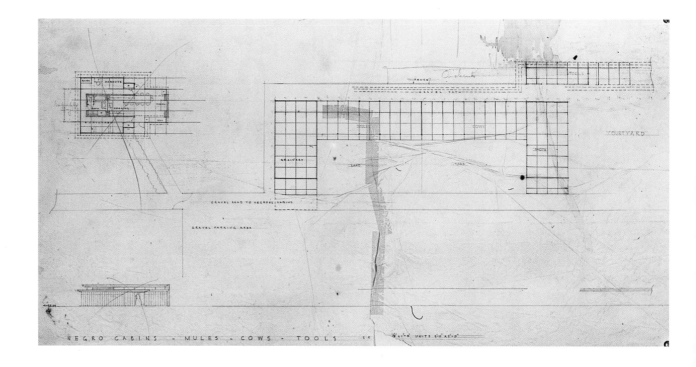

NEGRO CABINS - MULES - COWS - TOOLS

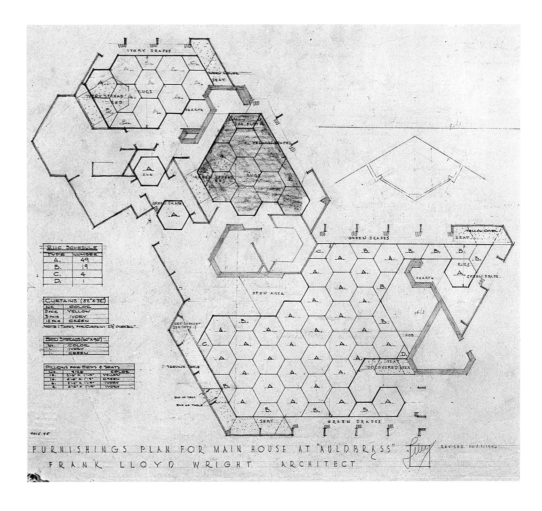

FIG. 91
FURNITURE LAYOUT
Auldbrass, main house showing pieced
carpet. Courtesy of the FLWA 4015.045

FOLLOWING PAGES
FIG. 92
STAFF CABINS
Auldbrass. Alan Weintraub/Arcaid, 2001

shown) together with larger quarters for a resident house-keeper. Otherwise its design remained essentially unchanged from its prewar state, although elevations showing inward- and outward-canting walls are more crisply drawn, and on one sheet the second floor has been crossed out, no doubt recording a later attempt to reduce its size.[14] Details for the long, hexagonal swimming pool show inward-sloped walls that would have amplified a visual effect of great depth.[15]

Additional drawings record minor revisions being suggested through much of 1947. A new site plan locates the cottage for house servants adjacent to the kitchen of the main house, and shows the kitchen extended by a newly added porch. The connecting driveways remained essential to the unity of the layout; a detail on the site plan shows how their lines would be sharpened by recessed stone gutters. Red gravel is specified at the gate by the caretaker's house and for the parking court of the guest house.[16]

What actual construction occurred during this second phase of work, between 1946 and 1948, remains unclear, and there may have been none. In late 1947 or early 1948, even design activities abruptly stopped once again. Wright telegraphed in January, 1948, "My dear Leigh: What's the matter?"[17] Stevens remained silent. Correspondence between the two ceased, for the time being, at least, and no evidence survives of any activity over the next few years. Stevens's failure to respond to Wright's telegram might reflect irritation at the publication of Auldbrass in a second *Architectural Forum* devoted to Wright's work; this January, 1948, issue appeared just before Wright telegraphed to ask what the problem might be.[18] As with the special issue of the *Forum* that appeared in 1938—indeed, as with most publications devoted to Wright's work during his lifetime—Wright himself selected projects to be included, supervised layouts and identified images, so there would have been little doubt as to who was responsible. No photographs were included—these would have required Stevens's cooperation—only draw-

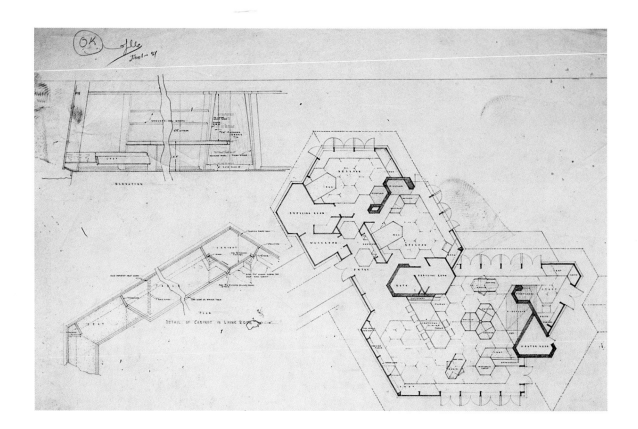

ings. But it violated Stevens's determination that nothing of the project would be published.

While publication of Auldbrass might have contributed to a temporary cessation of correspondence, it would seem unlikely to have precipitated the more drastic step of again abandoning the project. More probably this second pause (as it proved to be) was due to Stevens's second wife. Overwhelmed by the rough, unfinished character of the place, she had grown to dislike Auldbrass and hated living there. Stevens apparently lost confidence in her ability, or desire, to expend any effort toward its completion.[19] Part of his purpose in completing Auldbrass had been lost.

In the fall of 1948, Stevens was distracted by yet another adventure. Appointed as a Visiting Lecturer on Business Administration at Harvard, he began a teaching involvement there that was to last until his death in 1962.[20] Commuting to Cambridge, Massachusetts, he offered special seminars for other members of the faculty and tutored individual students.[21] His daughter reports that, "of all his achievements, Stevens was most proud of his professional connection at the Harvard Business School."[22]

At about the same time he began his involvement with Harvard, Stevens and his second wife agreed to a formal separation. She took up residence on board a private yacht he owned—it was moored in Miami, her place of residence until they were divorced in 1950.[23] Named Sea Mist, motorized and sixty-five feet long, its permanent crew of three—captain, deck hand, and steward—would stand at attention when Stevens boarded. It provided a rather more luxurious and ordered environment than Auldbrass ever did, and he frequently took it out for fishing trips of a week or more, escaping both the pressures of business and building (fig. 94).[24] It later offered a place of refuge for Stevens's next wife, too, until financial difficulties forced him to sell it in the mid 1950s, a loss he deeply regretted.

Stevens married his third wife, Nina Katherine Lunn, in 1950. They met in Havana, where she had gone for a holiday following the publication of her book, *Physical Attraction and Your Hormones; A Modern Guide to Beauty, Vitality, and Health*.[25] She and Stevens were married just after Christmas that same year, as soon as his most recent divorce was final.

Originally from Maine and reportedly the stepdaughter of Wallace H. White, Jr. (1877–1952), who served as the Republican Senator from Maine from 1931–1949, Nina Lunn moved in socially prominent circles in Long Island and among the plantations surrounding Auldbrass. She had been married twice herself and had three grown chil-

dren.[26] Reports that she thought of herself as a "glamour girl" and wanted to be in the movies are substantiated by the fact that she managed to obtain bit parts in at least two: *The Senator Was Indiscreet* (1947), in which she appeared for approximately 30 seconds as a shapely blond with an outrageous hat and fluttering eyes in the non-speaking part of "girl in the elevator," and as "guest" in *Up in Central Park* (1948).[27] Her brief movie career seems to have terminated about the time her stepfather's last term ended.

From the beginning of their relationship Nina had shown an active interest in Auldbrass, and she now set out to "make a nest there."[28] Upon her arrival—accompanied only by her eldest daughter, as it turned out, for Stevens had departed on one of his trips—she found the place unfinished and neglected, the kitchen hopelessly abandoned with no evidence of use. "The place is plumb deserted," the caretaker told her, adding that the last time Stevens's had gone away, he "didn't come back for near four years."[29] This would correspond with the period from 1942 to 1946, when construction had stopped and Stevens was otherwise involved.

Nina took a more aggressive stance than Stevens's second wife. She began to direct the workers herself, strug-

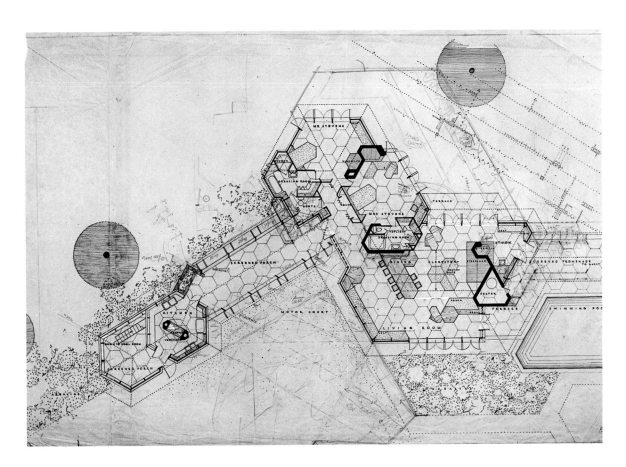

FIG. 95
PLAN OF MAIN HOUSE
Auldbrass. FLWA 4015.019

OPPOSITE
FIG. 96
SEATING ALCOVE
Auldbrass, living room of main house. FLWA

FIG. 97
SEATING ALCOVE
Auldbrass, living room of main house. FLWA

FOLLOWING PAGES
FIG. 98
SEATING ALCOVE
Auldbrass, alcove at far left, main
house. Anthony Peres, 2010

FIG. 99
MRS. STEVENS'S BEDROOM
Auldbrass, main house. Courtesy Jessica Stevens Loring

FIG. 100
SMALL BEDROOM
Auldbrass, main house. Anthony Peres, 2001

gling to reactivate the complicated and partly inoperative heating, hot water, and electrical systems. According to her own account, she engaged Stevens's son to help. He was then managing the local telephone company which his father had purchased, but had not earlier been involved in work at the plantation.[30] She soon began to campaign for other changes as well. The kitchen would do for servants, she decided, but was too remote for her own use. She demanded a smaller, more convenient "owners' kitchen," to be located somewhere within the house itself.[31] She also wanted the open pavilion linking the house with the detached kitchen enclosed, preferably with glass but at least with screen, so the staff could serve meals without passing through a place so unprotected from the elements. The awkwardness of operating the hinged glass doors along the perimeter of the house irritated her, as did the lack of terraces adjacent to the bedrooms. Feeling the living room too dark, she suggested further opening the clerestory by replacing its Wright-designed decorative wood panels with additional glass. And there were questions regarding the finishing of the interiors, in particular the furniture.

Stevens took Nina to Taliesin so they could discuss these matters with Wright, re-establishing communications after a period of some three years. In anticipation of their visit, Wright prepared a new furniture layout, dated June 1, 1951, that outlined how built-in seats and tables would relate with freestanding pieces to complete the architectural enclosure of the living room (fig. 93). Nina brought pictures showing how Auldbrass actually looked; things were not what Wright expected. The original copper foil on the roofs had long since disintegrated, the result of acid-producing leaves that fell in profusion each fall. It had been replaced by a conventional roof of tar and asphalt, an amorphous mass obscuring any trace of its original crystalline quality, and the entire surface had been covered with aluminum paint. A slightly later photograph suggests the impression this change would give (fig. 1, see pp. 2-3 and 128-129). Wright erupted, "I said positively NO aluminum!"[32]

How Wright reacted to other suggestions remains unknown, but on one drawing—the plan that had been prepared for publication in 1948—he recorded notes

FIG. 101
STUDY, MAIN HOUSE
Auldbrass. Courtesy Jessica Stevens Loring

FIG. 102
**STUDY, TOWARD LIVING ROOM,
MAIN HOUSE**
Auldbrass. Alan Weintraub/Arcaid, 2001

reflecting their discussion (fig. 95). A portion of the breezeway extending toward the future guest house was to be enclosed to create the owners' kitchen, and Stevens's study was to be converted to a small dining room. The roofed pavilion linking the main house to its detached kitchen was to be screened, and the entrance door shifted as a result, so one could enter the house more directly. The hinged glass doors opening from the bedrooms were to be replaced by sliding doors, and the terrace adjoining the living room was to be extended so it continued along these bedrooms as well.

While Wright's furniture had earlier been accepted by Stevens—he had already built a considerable quantity—Nina was clearly dissatisfied. Perhaps out of frustration, Wright suggested they contact Edward J. Wormley, a designer for the Dunbar Furniture Company.[33] Wormley's talents were warmly regarded by architects and designers. He was later described as "one of the most durable talents and most modest personalities in the field," and Edgar Kaufmann, jr. praised his designs.[34] Stevens and his wife contacted Wormley almost immediately, meeting with him in his New York office. They brought photographs of the living room without its Wright-designed pieces—Stevens had removed them in order to obtain a clearer view of the space to be refurnished. Not convinced by the stock items Wormley offered, they commissioned new pieces, and Wormley presented his designs in August 1951. He was known for his design of distinctive sofas,[35] and for Auldbrass he had designed two twelve-foot long lounges, angled so they joined at sixty degrees. They were to be positioned opposite the fireplace in the living room, taking the place of Wright's grouped hassocks. For the center of the room, he proposed a hexagonal coffee table with glass top and brass legs. These proved acceptable and Stevens authorized their fabrication.[36]

During this time, Wright prepared new drawings to show the architectural revisions agreed upon in June 1951.[37] He and Stevens continued to remain in touch, and their pattern of telegrams and missed meetings began again.[38] Meanwhile Nina continued to have other ideas. She disliked the red color of the concrete floors and the yellow-orange of the exposed wood—effectively every visible surface, except for the glass. She decided to substitute "the sky colors, the water colors, the whole family of them."[39] Wormley's lounges were to be upholstered with a tweed fabric in shades of aqua; raw silk in peacock blue was to cover a chair and ottoman; another shade of blue was selected for the banquettes (which had survived the reconfiguration); patterned linen in many colors was selected for other chairs, including several pieces by Wright which had been retained.

New estimates for Wright's pieced carpet "ran into thousands of dollars," which was judged too expensive. In its place, Nina substituted an even-textured cotton broadloom made by Karistan. Its colors were to be varied—deep copper for the entrance area, beige for the perimeter of the living room, white for the center, gray around the perimeter overlooking the wetlands, turquoise blue for her bedroom and white for his.[40] Draperies were added to soften outlines of the windows, and small cushions in various shades of blue purchased to adorn the lounges and chairs. Photographs of the living room taken later suggest the overall effect, with Wormley's soft, over-scaled lounges and oddly diminutive coffee table occupying their position of prominence (fig. 96). His clumsy, reductive reflection of Wright's flexible hexagonal module suggests that he failed to grasp much of the essence of Wright's design. The centrally placed lounges impeded the informal continuity that Wright had envisioned, and the fussiness of their tufted upholstery, together with the exaggerated delicacy of the brass-legged glass table, worked against the lodge-like atmosphere of the structure.

The patterned curtains and softly textured carpet installed by Nina completed what must have been a rather startling transformation (fig. 97). Photographs taken later of her bedroom (fig. 99) and of the small area behind the living room fireplace (fig. 101)—sometimes a study, sometimes a dining room—further convey impressions of colors, textures, and shapes at odds with their architectural setting. At some point the brick walls in the study/dining room, and both the brick and cypress walls in her bedroom, had been painted, so that a whole sea of Nina's "sky and water colors" prevailed. Stevens's bedroom seemed to partly escape these attempts at beautification; only the fireplace bricks were painted, leaving the cypress walls apparently untouched.

Other changes affected the farm buildings. Nina wanted more guest rooms so that she might entertain in style; as the guest house had not been built, she made changes to the caretaker's house, the saddle room and cook shed to achieve these ends and to relate them more closely to her transformed house. As she described:

I had ripped out all the nasty little corner cupboards and beds built into the angles of the cabins' rooms and I had the cabins made as gay and bright as possible. They had been painted on the inside, had windows over the sinks, and even a bathroom had been added under the long overhang. In addition I had installed new beds, chairs, a table and some dishes.

The main house looked beautiful. My carpets were gorgeous, so clean and fresh and colorful. The new furniture with its brilliant linen covers changed the whole room. The dark cavelike appearance had vanished! This was my room. I felt that I had created it, almost by myself.[41]

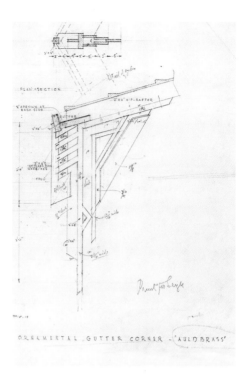

TOP
FIG. 102

**DETAIL OF ORNAMENTAL
PENDANT FOR MAIN HOUSE**

Auldbrass; noted in Frank Lloyd Wright's hand,
"print for Leigh." FLWA 4015.019

ABOVE
FIG. 103

DETAIL OF MAIN HOUSE

Auldbrass, showing ornamental pendant and
working down spouts. Courtesy Jessica Stevens Loring

RIGIHT
FIG. 104

RESTORED PORCH

Auldbrass, main house. Anthony Peres, 2010

LEFT
FIG. 105
FARM BUILDINGS AFTER FIRE
Auldbrass. Courtesy Joel Silver

OPPOSITE RIGHT
FIG. 106
FARM BUILDINGS AFTER FIRE
Auldbrass. Courtesy Jessica Stevens Loring

FAR OPPOSITE
FIG. 107
FAR CORNER OF CARETAKER'S HOUSE
Auldbrass, showing where fire was stopped. Courtesy Jessica Stevens Loring

FOLLOWING PAGES
FIG. 108
FARM BUILDINGS
Auldbrass, from main house with kennels at left and caretaker's house at far right.
Paul Rocheleau, 1992

Changes to the exteriors of the buildings were fewer in number and generally more sympathetic to Wright's original intentions. The most visible involved an attempt to correct the problem caused by the lack of copper for the distinctive downspouts. It had not been possible to build these elements that Wright had designed to articulate the corners of the broad eaves, and in their place conventional drainpipes had been installed. They gave the unfortunate impression of structural columns, badly compromising the sweep of the low, cantilevered overhangs. Copper was still difficult to obtain in 1951, so as a compromise, at Stevens's request, Wright designed ornamental wood pendants (fig. 102) to be suspended at each corner, between the working downspouts (fig. 103). Both downspouts and pendants were painted turquoise, presumably in emulation of patinated copper.

Letters from Stevens to Wright record other, more serious problems. While Stevens was at Auldbrass in March 1952, a fire destroyed significant portions of the farm buildings.[42] It began in a large, detached barn (not designed by Wright) that had been added beyond the hay barn (as it had come to be called), and it spread quickly to the machine shed and the hay barn itself. An excited brigade of volunteer fire fighters rushed to the scene, but discovered their pumps would not work. A bucket brigade was formed, and the roof linking the caretaker's house to the animal stalls and laundry was hacked down in an effort to contain the fire. This worked, saving the caretaker's house, stables, saddle room, cook shed, and kennels.[43] The main house and staff cabins were not affected, but the grand sweep of the farm buildings had been sadly reduced (fig. 105, 106, 107). Estimates for rebuilding proved prohibitive, and the buildings were not replaced, except for a small hexagonal shed, designed by Stevens, to contain electrical switches and store tools (fig. 109).[44]

In the fall of 1952, three of Wright's apprentices visited Auldbrass on their return from touring Florida Southern College, Wright's other major design in the area.[45] They

were impressed by what they described as the "sameness" of the components—the same materials, the same scale—prevalent throughout.[46] This perceptive understanding of the unity thus achieved, of the equality of parts thus demonstrated, seemed not to impress Nina. They were appalled by the changes she had made, and recalled Stevens apologizing in private for what had happened, saying it was "not Wright."[47]

Early in 1953, after ignoring warnings from her family that Stevens disliked her interference with his plantation, the intensity of his objections became clear. Arriving in New York from a vacation in Europe, Nina was telephoned by her brother who reported that Stevens would not allow her to return to Auldbrass. A confirming letter from Stevens arrived shortly: "[Auldbrass] holds no interest for you. It is back where it was before our marriage. I forbid you to go there and I shall send all of your things wherever you wish."[48]

A period of separation followed, no doubt encouraging a renewed, but still tempered, cordiality between Stevens and Wright. Stevens had asked if Dean Donald K. David, of the Harvard Business School, might visit Wright at Taliesin West. "His primary interest is education," he wrote to Wright, "and I have told him that it was essential that he see your marvelous system of education in operation . . .".[49] Wright responded that he would welcome Dean David, adding, "And glad to hear from you."[50] Stevens apparently accompanied Dean David on his visit, and he felt greatly complimented by Wright's characterization of his patronage, as his next letter to Wright revealed:

> Quite the nicest compliment ever paid this old engineer was your remark about his appreciation of design. I would like to make it official and would you mind writing me a note in your own handwriting—which will really make it official—confirming the verbal pronouncement. . . .
> I enjoyed my day with you in Taliesin very much. It is always a great inspiration.[51]

Wright responded (typed, not handwritten, but signed with his full name; for Wright, this was a mark of respect), "Dear Leigh: As a client your perspicacity and appreciation goes high in our experience. Seldom do we see a man of your wide experience so aware of values in the art of Architecture. More power to such."[52]

Even without Nina, Stevens was not above making changes of his own, as his previous efforts during construction had shown. One such change involved the implementation of a landscaping plan Stevens had earlier asked Thomas D. Church, the prominent landscape architect, to prepare. Church, whose work at the time was primarily in California, was noted for his flexible approach to garden design, and for his incorporation of asymmetrical, freely-disposed curvelinear elements.[53] At the time of the commission, Stevens agreed with Nina in wanting to add decorative shrubs, but the sheep they kept to help maintain the vast lawn tended to eat any decorative plants, adding to the problem of landscape design.[54]

Church submitted his initial proposal in April 1952, but nothing further was done at that time. He had suggested a low brick wall, laid out to describe a hexagon around the immediate area of the house. Like a ha-ha, this would keep out the sheep without impeding distant views, and would have the added advantage of defining a clear area for the non-indigenous plants to be added.[55] Now, without Nina in April 1953, Stevens pressed Wright for his comments on the scheme, sending him a copy for review with the added encouragement, "as Church says, it's subordinate to Wright's great concept. . ." (fig 110, 111).[56] Wright's reaction was predictable. "Dear Lee," he tersely responded, "The Church layout is here. What now."[57] Stevens tried again: "I need your comments on Church's wall badly please."[58] Finally, in June, Wright responded more directly. Sketched on Church's plan were less formal, more flowing shapings of low walls and planting beds; the varied hexagonal shapes, more sensitively manipulated, reinforced and extended the architectural forms of the house to much better effect.[59] Evidently neither Stevens nor Church appreciated the difference, and in the end Church's scheme was implemented with few, if any, changes. An undated exterior view of the approach to the house shows the hexagonal wall in the foreground (see fig. 1, pp.2-3 and pp. 128-129), and a view toward the living room at the back includes a decorative pool that Church designed and that was added later, a curious feature for a house located on the edge of wet lowlands (fig. 112, 113).

At some point, Stevens and Nina ended what turned out to be a relatively brief period of separation, and Nina was allowed to return to Auldbrass. To judge by new activity there, this would have been during the summer of 1953. It was then that Wright revived his plan for a housekeeper's cottage, now worked out in greater detail (fig. 115). Nina had long demanded proper accommodations for servants; as Stevens himself had once explained, Wright expected that six would be necessary to run the main house. To be conveniently located beyond the kitchen, this two-bedroom cottage might have extended its lines, but seemed never to have fully captured Wright's imagination, or have been fully integrated with the other buildings. To the degree it was developed, as noted on the drawings, "All details of board walls, partitions and sash, same as in main house. Roof same as main house to pitch same as other cabins."

The next activity involved a more complete enclosure of the roofed connection linking the kitchen with the main

FIG. 109
SWITCH HOUSE
Auldbrass. Courtesy Jessica Stevens Loring

house. It had earlier been enclosed with simple, conventionally vertical panels of insect screening;[60] now a scheme of glazing was devised in order to provide a more formal area for dining. The plan for angled bay windows that Wright submitted in August 1953, had first been sketched on an earlier drawing, again offering a record, it seems, of his quick response.[61]

Neither the housekeeper's cottage nor the new dining room enclosure were built at this time, nor was any immediate modification made to the breezeway beyond the study so that it might accommodate an "owners' kitchen." But other, more wide-ranging changes were now realized. One involved the low, swampy field behind the main house where a previous owner had long before raised indigo.[62] Ambitiously, Stevens decided to transform this field into a real lake, so that boats from the house might reach the Combahee River and even the ocean, thus providing a greatly enhanced opportunity for fishing. The lake would also have defined a clearer line between land and water where before none had existed, creating an approximation of the shoreline Wright had once imagined.

Stevens's scheme for the lake reflects the same determination that he showed in an ambitious project in India, begun around 1954. Under the sponsorship of the Ford Foundation and at the invitation of the Indian government, Stevens joined a team of experts touring India with the purpose of offering advice on how small-scale industries might be encouraged.[63] He suggested harnessing the power of bullocks hitched to a central wheel, to be worked like a mill, in order to solve two immediate problems: water supply (the turning motion could be made to power a pump) and electricity (it could also power a generator). He further proposed that the power generated be used to operate village carpentry and metalwork shops as a spur to local industry, and he worked with American brick companies to improve the quality of Indian production of that basic building material. By 1958, he had managed to put one of the bullock-powered pumps into operation, and he is pictured together with Nehru and other onlookers. (fig. 117).[64]

Stevens's parallel project at Auldbrass, which, one might think, could have been readily accomplished, proved more elusive. To create the lake required not only the deepening of the low field behind the house, but also the construction of a canal to bring water from the river as well as provide for the passage of boats. The canal was completed in 1955, and a pump was installed at its head to fill the lake. At first the water seeped away through the

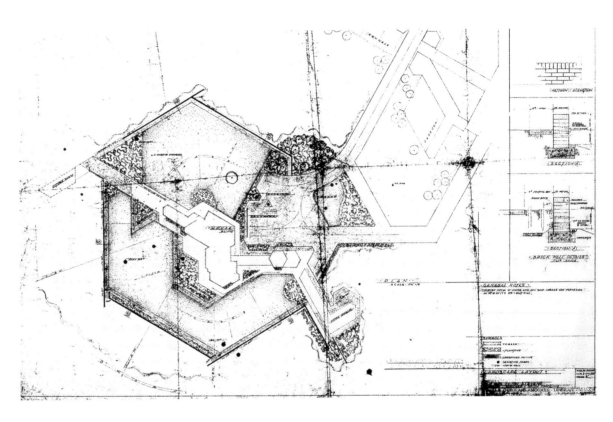

ABOVE
FIG. 111
**THOMAS CHURCH,
LANDSCAPING PLAN
FOR MAIN HOUSE**

Auldbrass. Courtesy Jessica Stevens Loring
and Joel Silver

LEFT
FIG. 110
**MAIN HOUSE WITH SHEEP GRAZING
IN FOREGROUND**

Auldbrass. Courtesy Joel Silver

FIG. 112
LIVING ROOM
Auldbrass, added owner's kitchen at left and decorative pool in foreground. Courtesy Jessica Stevens Loring

porous soil, but eventually constant pumping overcame this problem. The resulting lake was greatly admired, but the pump soon broke, the water dissipated, and the scheme was abandoned.[65]

With equal zeal, Stevens continued to undertake other tasks, usually with better results. He worked strenuously to make Auldbrass into a working plantation, but on his own terms of experimentation, raising livestock and crops in ways unlike those of his neighbors. These activities he gradually expanded into more remote areas of the plantation, but many of his fields have since reverted to forest, so no immediately visible trace remains. His sheep barns, too, have dis-

appeared. The cattle he raised included Brahma bulls, and at another location he had what he called a "pig parlor." He grew crops to provide food for these animals, and elsewhere crops in what he called "provision fields" to supply the plantation itself.[66] The extensive chicken coops, of course, remained a visible part of the Wright-designed complex.

According to his daughter, he trained himself for these endeavors by studying books on farming, amassing a small library to achieve this end. Among those books he consulted was *Five Acres and Independence*, aimed at a smaller operation (Auldbrass encompassed 4,253 acres) but including comforting, Wright-like encouragement:

Which, think you, is the better citizen, the man who pays rent for a hall room, a hotel suite, or a 'flat,' or the one who owns a self-supporting rural home and therein rears a family of sons and daughters by the labors of his head and his hands and their assistance?[67]

According to Nina, Stevens came close to achieving his end of independence. She reports that everything served for a lavish Christmas Eve dinner was produced at Auldbrass "except the sugar, salt, and coffee."[68] But ultimately this, too, came apart. The effort of maintaining so intensive an operation was rendered impossible by his demanding business involvements. One of his plantation

workers recalled that things went well enough when Stevens was in residence, but not when he was away.[69]

When not overseeing work on his plantation, Stevens occupied himself by making changes to the buildings, but now, in the mid 1950s, with no record of any involvement by Wright. He enlarged his bathroom, extended the detached servants' kitchen to include the screened porch that lay beyond (fig. 118), removed the stove from the kitchen's center, and altered the layouts of the saddle room (which became more of an office) and the caretaker's house. To counter the dampness of the exposed concrete floors in the extended servants' kitchen, he added a layer of linoleum.[70]

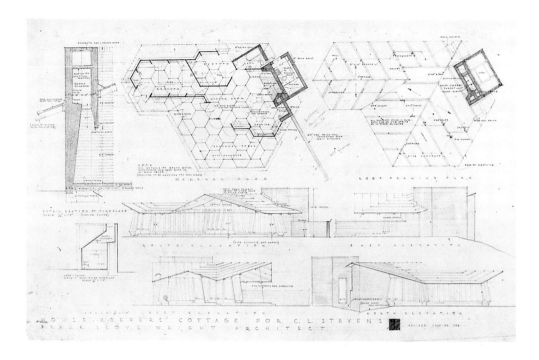

LEFT
FIG. 115
**PLANS, ELEVATIONS, AND
DETAILS OF HOUSEKEEPER'S
COTTAGE**
Auldbrass. FLWA 4026.002

BELOW
FIG. 116
COTTAGE
Auldbrass. Courtesy Jessica Stevens Loring

Nina more than kept up with her husband in altering Auldbrass. The hearths of the four fireplaces in the main house were raised in an attempt to prevent them from smoking, and small air conditioning units were positioned in various rooms. Although Stevens later demanded that the fireplace alterations be removed, it would fall to a later owner to realize this correction. With the air conditioning, Stevens seemed to be in greater accord. By then he decided to occupy Auldbrass for much of the year rather than only in winter, and summers proved unbearably hot, as earlier owners of plantations had long ago known. Mechanical engineers were consulted in an effort to install a centrally powered, more permanent system than possible with individual window units, but the engineers were unable to devise an arrangement that could be effectively concealed, and Stevens, not wanting to destroy the integrity of the design, dropped the idea. Vertical aluminum blinds were added behind the glass doors to reflect as much of the sun's heat as possible, but it seems the house was never as comfortable as Stevens wished during the hot months.[71]

Whatever the changes, Nina remained dissatisfied, always fighting with the house. Obviously she wanted the very type of plantation Wright and Stevens were determined to avoid: a place of refined domesticity, conventionally charming, with an affected style suggestive of an

earlier time. Repeatedly she asked Stevens to buy or build her a house of her own, one which she could decorate as she chose, but with the understanding that Wright not be involved. Briefly Stevens seemed willing to grant her request, and they consulted with Alfred Browning Parker, a follower of Wright's who practiced in Florida.[72] It was an intriguing choice: a Wrightian architect known for his accommodating skills and for his comfortable houses. In the end, however, Stevens neither bought nor built a house for Nina, although Stevens's daughter recalls that Parker became involved with some of the changes at Auldbrass itself. What these changes were remains uncertain. Evidently, Parker was not involved with the second (or "owners") kitchen added under the covered passage, which was to connect with the future guest house; Nina describes it as her own doing, and its awkward details support this claim (fig. 119, 121). Nor, it seems, was Parker involved in the design of a small residentially-scaled building, located where the housekeeper's cottage was to have been. Nina relates how Stevens built it without outside advice, fitting out its interior with tiled enclosures to house her poodle dogs (she admits to having around thirty at the time).[73] The possibility of including some accomodations for household staff was also mentioned but it was never finished, and remained for many years a ghostly, desolate presence (fig. 116).[74]

By late 1956, Stevens's displeasure over his third wife's meddling was again evident. He spoke of his "sense of failure" at not being able to make Auldbrass what he wanted, partly because of her interference; on one occasion, he refused to meet her guests, saying, "you do it—it's your house now."[75] Wright's reaction to her changes would not have helped the situation. She showed him pictures—perhaps unwisely—when she and Stevens met with him at his Plaza Hotel suite in New York in March, 1957. These may be among those now retained in the Frank Lloyd Wright Archives (see figs. 96, 97). To her great dismay, Wright was immediately critical.[76] Still convinced of the rightness of her work, she invited Wright and his wife to visit Auldbrass, no doubt partly in an attempt to win his approval. It was proposed that they come after a lecture Wright was scheduled to give in Atlanta; Stevens offered to send a car, or a plane if his guests preferred.[77] Yet unexpected events were to prevent this visit, for in May Wright received his Baghdad opera house commission, and he cancelled his lecture engagement to travel to that city instead.[78]

Stevens and Nina were divorced in June 1957.[79] To judge from her account, it was again, like the separation in 1953, a sudden decision in which she played no part.[80] In July 1957, Stevens married for the fourth time, to Barbara Berger Honeyman, of Portland, Oregon. His daughter remembered that this fourth wife had been mar-

FIG. 117

STEVENS IN INDIA

C. Leigh Stevens (third from left) with Nehru (second from left). Punjab Photo Service, New Delhi; courtesy Jessica Stevens Loring

FIG. 119
BEDROOMS
Auldbrass, main house, with added owners' kitchen at left. Courtesy Joel Silver, ca. 1979

FOLLOWING PAGES
FIG. 120
MAIN HOUSE
Auldbrass, with kitchen porch in center and parking court at right. Anthony Peres, 2001

ried at least twice before. Unlike Nina, she left no lively record of her life at Auldbrass, nor any indication of what her involvement with the plantation, if any, might have been. Whatever changes occurred at Auldbrass during the next five years went unrecorded, and there is no evidence of any significant alterations to the buildings themselves. Stevens's daughter remembers only that this fourth wife added the odd decorative pool (that Church had earlier suggested) behind the master bedroom.[81]

The second period of building at Auldbrass was drawing rapidly to a close. Frank Lloyd Wright died in Phoenix in April 1959, having never made a second visit to the plantation he designed. Stevens died of a heart attack in Cambridge, Massachusetts, in October, 1962.[82] At the time he was still working to establish his bullock-powered generators and pumps in India, proposing that some 15,000 acres of land be temporarily acquired for that purpose, then redistributed to Indian farmers in small plots.[83] His other major project at the time was the establishment of the Student Educational

Loan Fund (SELF), a subsidized loan program to provide student aid from private sources,[84] and a model for programs now widely found in the United States.

Whatever Nina's misgivings regarding Wright, and however bitter her later views of Stevens might have been, she was able to perceive remarkable qualities in both. As she wrote some years after her divorce,

Ordinary men are fearful of being different; afraid to break a pattern or to ignore tradition. Not these two. Both believed their creative ability led to greater and greater achievement. What Wright dared to do for architecture, Leigh did for industry.[85]

Both Wright and Stevens were also dedicated to building, and theirs was an essential relationship, for architects without such determined clients achieve little. And however problematic some of Stevens's own changes to Auldbrass might have been, he remained dedicated to honoring essential aspects of Wright's concept, and to completing the vision of a newly constituted southern plantation it embodied.

CHAPTER 6

JESSICA STEVENS LORING AND THE SURVIVAL OF AULDBRASS

MAIN HOUSE
Auldbrass, with farm buildings in distance
at far right. Anthony Peres, 2001

FIG. 125
MAIN GATEWAY
Auldbrass, with kennels at right and adapt-
ed farm buildings at left. Anthony Peres, 2001

The story of Auldbrass might all too easily have ended with the death of Leigh Stevens in 1962. Neither of his children had ever lived there, and neither they nor his widow (his fourth wife, but only since 1957) could have felt close to its history, or so it might be argued. And how reasonable it must have seemed for his heirs to sell the property outright and escape from its overburdening responsibility, entrusting its future to any buyer, however disinterested, so they might be free of its care. Yet some of the same determination that drove Stevens to pursue his ideal image of place seemed also to have affected his daughter, Jessica Stevens Loring. Through her efforts and those of her husband, Stanton D. Loring, the story of Auldbrass continued.

Settling the estate proved complicated, as would be expected in the wake of Stevens's complicated financial dealings. He had named the manager of his Savannah Lumber Corporation as primary executor, leaving everything to his son (Clifton Delmar), daughter (Jessica) and fourth wife (Barbara Berger Honeyman Stevens). Others made claims, including his second and third wives, and an outstanding mortgage on the property further complicated matters.[1] Stevens's daughter helped sort things out, later describing her efforts as "a true case study in management, such as the lectures Leigh regularly gave at the Harvard Business School."[2]

Stevens's widow soon moved to California, and early in 1964 the Lorings purchased her interest in Auldbrass. Two years later Jessica Stevens Loring began living there

FIG. 128

CEREMONIES TO MARK LISTING OF AULDBRASS ON NATIONAL REGISTER

Left to right: Lt. Governor Brantley Harvey, Cynthia Cole, Jessica Stevens Loring, Stanton Loring. Courtesy Jessica Stevens Loring

for extended periods to better manage the estate, and in 1970, through an exchange of property with her brother, she and her husband became sole owners of Auldbrass. They took up permanent residence the very next year, but resuscitating the plantation proved no easy matter. Stevens's livestock had long since been sold by the executors of his will, and the cleared fields had been leased, or allowed to revert to woodlands. Fewer than 200 of the 4,253 acres were still under cultivation, and on these, as they gradually took over the leases, the Lorings raised corn and soybeans. Stevens had raised these crops as feed for his livestock, but the Lorings, having elected to dispense with that component of the plantation, raised these crops for cash. Yet benefits were limited. As Mrs. Loring explained, "I was proud that I made a profit, though I did not make a living."[3]

Whatever the financial constraints, the Lorings struggled to maintain the estate as Stevens had left it (fig. 126). In addition to the main house, the expansive development still included kennels, the manager's office with adjacent living quarters (earlier adapted by Stevens from the saddle room and cook shed), stables, nearby storage, the caretaker's house across the main driveway (fig. 127, 129), and, still more distant, two staff cabins, all designed by Frank Lloyd Wright. Even though these buildings were modestly sized—the main house not quite 4,000 square feet, and the others remaining just over 6,300 square feet—their extended disposition across the property, and their unconventional construction, made upkeep difficult.[4]

Finding reliable help in running the estate, and paying for that help, compounded the problems of living at Auldbrass. For the house alone, as earlier noted, Wright had suggested that a minimum of six servants would be necessary; neither Stevens nor his daughter were able to operate at this scale. Dependable farm workers were also scarce, and few, it seemed, lived permanently at Auldbrass as originally intended. During their years of stewardship, the Lorings kept in residence at least one in service, comparatively luxurious for the time, but still insufficient to provide a sense of ease. For while Wright had succeeded in challenging the conventional order of a southern plantation, his new order was already outdated by changes in the American labor market after World War II, and his creation nearly as endangered as its antebellum forebears.

Contributing to the fragility of Wright's vision were compromises and changes that had beset Auldbrass from its beginnings. The main guest house, aviary, and swimming pool had never been built. The grain and hay barn, chicken sheds, mule and horse sheds, laundry, dairy, and machine shed had never been rebuilt following the fire of 1952. The cottage that was at best a pale imitation of Wright, the tool shed designed by Stevens himself, and garden elements added by Thomas Church compromised the visual unity Wright sought. Changes wrought by Nina Lunn Stevens to the residential units further detracted from an idealized image of rustic splendor.

The Lorings coped with these compromises to the degree their energies and finances would permit, concentrating effort on the house itself. They began extensive repairs during the summer of 1971 by replacing the roof and upgrading the mechanical systems. They gave careful attention to smaller details, too; thus coatings of liquid cre-

FIG. 129
COOK SHED

Auldbrass, stables and caretaker's house beyond at left. Courtesy Jessica Stevens Loring

FIG. 130

ENTRANCE TO CARETAKER'S HOUSE

Auldbrass, with portion of secondary gateway through farm buildings at right. Courtesy Jessica Stevens Loring

osote so essential in maintaining the honey color of the cypress that both Wright and Stevens had wanted were again regularly applied (fig. 130). Inside, some of Nina's offending changes were reversed, or at least neutralized. Draperies and vertical aluminum blinds added in the living room were removed, reopening the expansive vistas so essential to the perception of Wrightian space (fig. 133, 134, 136). Removing paint from brick in the two bedrooms, and from the cypress in Mrs. Stevens's bedroom, the smaller of the two, loomed as too great a task, but the brick was at least repainted so it recalled the original color, thus establishing better harmony within the architectural setting (fig. 131). What was originally known as Mrs. Stevens's bedroom, the smaller of the two, had, by then, come to be called "the wives's bedroom" by the Lorings.[5]

The Lorings had also to deal with curious visitors who appeared unannounced. For while Auldbrass had never been widely published, it was known to architects and students, and they sought it out as they do all Wright's works,

however remote. For many owners of Wright properties, or indeed for many owners of any famous buildings, this constitutes a hated invasion. Yet the Lorings felt differently. They resolved to welcome those dedicated enough to find the plantation and to provide the tour routinely requested.[6] This was often far from convenient. In her diary, Mrs. Loring recorded how one group called her down from an oak tree where she had been in the midst of trimming away dead branches. More often, wandering unbidden across the grounds, they came upon her as she was working somewhere in the extensive garden. But they all got invited in.

Some visits yielded welcome moments, as when Herbert Jacobs, another of Wright's clients, happened by and declared the main room at Auldbrass "one of Frank Lloyd Wright's best."[7] William Allin Storrer stayed for almost a week, photographing everywhere. Visitations increased after he published the resulting guide to Wright buildings; to help respond to these further pressures, the Lorings produced

ABOVE
FIG. 131
**MRS. STEVENS'S
BEDROOM, MAIN HOUSE**
Auldbrass. Courtesy Jessica Stevens Loring

FOLLOWING PAGES
FIG. 132
LARGE BEDROOM, MAIN HOUSE
Auldbrass, showing bedroom fireplace.
Alan Weintraub/Arcaid, 2001

a handsome brochure featuring the arrow motif of the clerestory windows on its cover.[8] In 1976, St. Helena's Episcopal Church, in Beaufort, included Auldbrass on its tour of plantations; over 400 visitors came, many from distant locations and many with knowledge of Wright's work. Auldbrass continued to be a featured part of their later tours.

By 1976, the Lorings' generosity in opening the doors of Auldbrass had made the plantation visible in a way it never was before. No wonder the Governor of South Carolina, James B. Edwards, selected it as the appropriate site to welcome an important addition to Yemassee's economy, the LeCreuset cookware company, which originally chose the area for a manufacturing facility.[9] But, by 1976 Auldbrass was becoming too great a burden for the Lorings to bear much longer, and they sought some means of more permanent protection. Together with Cynthia Cole, the historic preservation planner with Lowcounty Council of Governments, they worked to place Auldbrass on the National Register of Historic Places. The Lt. Governor of South Carolina attended ceremonies marking its official listing (fig. 128).[10] Being on the National Register carries little real authority, but the honor at least imparts a mark of official recognition essential to most preservation efforts, and it was an effective way to begin. In 1979, after long seeking an appropriate buyer, the Lorings sold Auldbrass to Boise Cascade, a timber company they hoped would care for the buildings.

During their seventeen years of stewardship, the Lorings had maintained the estate with special understanding. No radical alterations had been made, and the architectural integrity of Wright's design had been preserved. Sensitive to broader meanings, they understood how the buildings themselves needed to remain part of their spacious site, and they included in the sale some 2,400 acres of surrounding land, so that Auldbrass could continue to be experienced as it had been designed.

Boise Cascade, described by Mrs. Loring as the purchaser of record, behaved in a manner reminiscent of ear-

ABOVE
FIG. 136
LIVING ROOM SEATING ALCOVE
Auldbrass, main house. Courtesy Joel Silver,
ca. 1979

OPPOSITE
FIG. 137
LIVING ROOM, MAIN HOUSE
Auldbrass, with light sconces suspended
above built-in sofa. Anthony Peres, 2002

lier dealings with the property, for ownership was almost immediately transferred to another entity, the Westvaco Corporation.[11] Retaining most of the estate's then 2,400 acres of woodlands and open fields for their own use, Westvaco, in turn, sold the buildings together with a small parcel of land to a group of local hunters who used the house and grounds as a lodge. The real estate company handling the original sale from the Lorings to Boise Cascade had perceived this dual potential of the property; their sales brochure for Auldbrass carried the caption, "A Superb Land & Timber Investment in a Sportsman's Paradise."[12]

The hunters, who had established their informal hunt club by 1981, found management of their newly acquired buildings difficult, and they fell gradually into ruin. Left untreated, the cypress turned dark gray and seemed on the verge of irreversible decay. The glass doors began to loosen from their hinges, window panes were broken, screen panels torn, and the ventilating panels along the perimeter of the floor became inoperable. Subject to the ever increasing weight imposed by added layers of roofing, the eaves began to sag. Inside, scorched, blackened areas of exposed wood sheathing recorded ferocious fires

that seemed almost to have escaped their hearths. Various creatures, including raccoons, rats, and bees, nested within. With these abuses, Auldbrass soon assumed the appearance of an abandoned plantation (figs. 138, 139, 140, 142, 143), but somehow, from a distance, it still retained a sense of integrity.

The Lorings had taken with them the moveable furniture designed by Wright, together with record prints of the working drawings. These now seemed of little need to the future of the house itself. Pieces were donated to the American Wing of the Metropolitan Museum of Art in 1981, and the record prints of Wright's drawings were deposited in the Avery Architectural Library at Columbia University.[13] Later that same year, remaining pieces were auctioned at Sotheby's in New York.[14]

Eventually things at Auldbrass began to change once again. Wright's buildings were not well suited to the hunters' needs, and they offered to donate them to Clemson University for an architectural restoration center. They preferred to erect a new, standardized building a short distance away and closer to the road. It would provide more convenient lodgings for their activities.[15]

To what degree the hunters were particularly concerned about preserving Wright's buildings is unclear, but other people in the area seemed to be, and they may have brought pressure to bear. It seems more likely too, that financial concerns played a part in efforts to transfer ownership. Reportedly the hunters had paid Westvaco $100,000 for their parcel of land together with the buildings, putting up $2000 in cash and covering the remainder with an unassumable farm loan.[16] At the time they offered the buildings to Clemson University, tax laws would have allowed significant benefits. Yet after studying their options, the university determined costs for such a center would be too great, and the offer was not accepted.

Assisting the hunters in determining the worth of their proposed donation was Donna Ratchford Butler, a Savannah appraiser who specialized in historic properties.[17] Recognizing the importance of Wright's design and its setting, she believed it would be best to transfer ownership of Auldbrass with an easement in place to protect those components. She sought advice from John Trask, then President of the Beaufort County Open Land Trust, who agreed to negotiate such an easement. As is typical for not-for-profit entities holding these easements, a significant cash donation would be required to support ongoing enforcement.

It was determined to seek a responsible buyer willing to make the cash donation as well as undertake required maintenance and restoration as specified by the easement. Yet as

a ruin, Auldbrass offered little but burdensome responsibility, and there would be few with the means and imagination to rescue an apparant folly, however great its designer. Further, time was not on their side. In order for the hunters to realize maximum tax benefits in the transfer of the property, a package had to be assembled before the end of the calendar year, when changes in state laws would cause tax deductions to be based on the actual value rather than the appraised value of the property. Because the easement would restrict conditions of ownership, the sale price would be significantly reduced. Seeking assistance in identifying a buyer as quickly as possible, Trask turned to a longtime friend well-positioned to help: Thomas M. Schmidt.[18]

Schmidt's connection with Wright properties was by then well known. As Director of the Western Pennsylvania Conservancy, he guided the stewardship of Fallingwater, one of Wright's most famous buildings which its owner, Edgar Kaufmann, jr., had given to the Conservancy (together with an endowment) so that it might be permanently open to the public. Not long after assuming responsibility for Fallingwater, Schmidt had begun efforts to establish what eventually became the Frank Lloyd Wright Building Conservancy, an organization dedicated to the preservation of all Wright properties.[19]

The appeal to Schmidt was well received, and late in the summer of 1986 he visited Auldbrass to discuss options and inspect the property.[20] That fall, in its early stages of

FIG. 142
DOG KENNELS
Auldbrass. Courtesy Joel Silver, ca. 1986

FIG. 143
STAFF CABIN
Auldbrass. Courtesy Joel Silver, ca. 1979

FOLLOWING PAGES
FIG. 144
MAIN HOUSE
Auldbrass, with dining room enclosure at
left and restored pergola at right.
Anthony Peres, 2001

formation, the Frank Lloyd Wright Building Conservancy held a meeting in Los Angeles. One of the speakers was Joel Silver, the Hollywood producer who two years earlier had bought another Wright property in need: the Storer house. Designed for a small Los Angeles site in 1923 and completed in 1924, it, too, had suffered from indignities over the years, and its experimental structure of masonry blocks was every bit as resistant to conventional management as was the inventive wood construction of Auldbrass. Yet over these impediments Silver gave every evidence of triumphing, working intensively with a team of restoration architects and builders, so that by 1986 he could present his accomplishments to the assembled group of Wright enthusiasts.[21] On the evening following his talk, Silver held a reception in the Storer house so that all could see his work firsthand, and his special dedication to Wright was further revealed.

The following morning Schmidt telephoned Silver to suggest that he consider rescuing Auldbrass as he had the Storer house. Silver asked what the price might be, and Schmidt recalls that he suggested a donation of $100,000.[22] Silver,

who had paid about the same amount for individual pieces of furniture, became intrigued; "You mean I can get a Frank Lloyd Wright plantation for what I paid for a table?" Schmidt recalls him saying.[23] He had long wanted a weekend retreat, and while filming in Puerto Vallarta had briefly considered buying there before being discouraged by complications of landownership in Mexico; South Carolina would not pose this problem. The story of Auldbrass was about to continue.

During these dealings and in the years that followed, as the fortunes of Auldbrass changed yet again, the Lorings remained watchful, hoping that its imagined glories might somehow be realized. Their actual connection to the place continued as well. For when they sold Auldbrass together with much of its land in 1979, they retained that part of the plantation known as the Old Combahee tract, some 1,862 acres of timberlands with outer boundaries that have remained unchanged since 1754. There, in 1997, on a bluff overlooking Izards Creek as it flows toward the Combahee River, they built a small weekend house and again became residents on a former part of the plantation.[24]

JOEL SILVER AND THE COMPLETION OF AULDBRASS

F rank Lloyd Wright believed all buildings in active use
would continue to evolve in a manner analogous to living organisms. Thus no building is ever really finished
in an absolute sense. Apart from those in which he himself
lived, surely no building by Wright better exemplifies this
than Auldbrass. And no owner of a Wright building better
appreciates Wright's outlook in this regard than Joel Silver,
who acquired Auldbrass in 1986 and began immediately
to pursue what he has come to see as a noble, but unending, quest: completion of the plantation (fig. 145). Joining
him in this endeavor has been his wife, Karyn. She visited
Auldbrass early on, while working for Silver, and since their
marriage in 1999, it has become a joint effort.[1]

Even the act of purchase was unusually complicated.
Following Thomas Schmidt's suggestion that he consider buying the property, Silver visited it for himself in October, 1986.
He knew something of its condition from photographs that he
had studied, so was not unduly discouraged by what he saw,
but he also had some idea of what its restoration was likely
to cost, and realized that the suggested donation of
$100,000 was not the great bargain it might seem. In giving
it careful consideration, he discussed the feasibility of rescue
with Eric Lloyd Wright, Wright's grandson, who had worked
with Silver in restoring the Storer house. Silver also examined
the original drawings at Taliesin West and met with Bruce
Brooks Pfeiffer, Director of the Frank Lloyd Wright Archives
who, as a former apprentice in the Taliesin Fellowship,
brought unique insights to questions of restoration.

FIG. 149
MAIN HOUSE
Auldbrass, showing restored kitchen porch.
Anthony Peres, 2001

FOLLOWING PAGES
FIG.150
LIVING ROOM, MAIN HOUSE
Auldbrass. Anthony Peres, 2001

Meanwhile, negotiations over the scale of the property, and the conditions of its transfer, continued. Joining Donna Butler, John Trask, and Thomas Schmidt in reaching an agreement were John Meffert, Director of the Southeast Regional Office of the National Trust for Historic Preservation; R. Angus Murdoch, Executive Director, Historic Charleston Foundation; and William Mixon, spokesman for the hunters' group. Silver agreed to the conditions of the easement, conditions that restricted any changes he might make to the Wright-designed buildings and provided for ongoing review of the property. Thus major aspects of its restoration would be strictly monitored. But as Silver soon learned, the $100,000 he was prepared to offer would cover only the donation to the Land Trust. No portion would be allocated toward the outstanding loan of $98,000, all of which would fall to Silver. Further, he had come to realize that the small amount of land being sold with the buildings was insufficient to guarantee a proper setting, yet acquiring additional land would further increase his costs.[2]

At the time Silver was in the early stages of his phenomenally successful career, with his greatest successes yet to come. Having already spent heavily in the restoration of the Storer house, he had foresight of what might lie ahead with Auldbrass, and he must also have questioned the wisdom of embarking on a second such venture so soon after the first. But his producer's vision enabled him to see what Auldbrass might become, and he wanted it. First, however, he had to negotiate his donation to the Land Trust (a frequent occurrence in such dealings). He was willing to offer $50,000, but only if additional land would be included. To this the hunters agreed so as to bring Silver's total to 55 acres, but for this land they would ask $10,000, prompting him to lower his donation accordingly. He also covered the outstanding loan of $98,000. This brought total acquisition costs to $148,000, a very small fraction of what he would ultimately spend on his restoration of the plantation. He closed on the property in mid-December 1986.[3]

FIG. 151
LIVING ROOM, MAIN HOUSE
Auldbrass, looking toward entrance and
bedrooms. Anthony Peres, 2010

Surely no more appropriate buyer for Auldbrass than Joel Silver could have been found. Early on, while growing up in South Orange, New Jersey, he had been impressed by a house designed by Taliesin Associated Architects, Wright's successor firm, and became drawn to Wright's work.[4] Later, while a student at New York University's film school, he encountered another fan: Tobias Mostel, the son of actor Zero Mostel. Together the two students studied everything on Wright they could find, beginning with the collection of books owned by Tobias's father. The elder Mostel had acquired them through his editor, Ben Raeburn, Wright's editor at Horizon Press.[5] Silver's fascination with Wright grew over the years that followed.

Like Wright and Stevens before him, Silver left college before obtaining his degree. He moved to Los Angeles in 1975, where he worked at various jobs related to the film industry. In the spring of 1977, his situation began to stabilize when he entered the employ of Lawrence Gordon, an independent film producer. Although he twice left Gordon's employ for other positions—first, in 1979, to be a production vice-president for Universal, then, around 1980, to be an executive vice-president at Polygram—each time he returned. In 1984, well experienced and confident of his own abilities, he founded Silver Pictures and began to produce such phenomenally successful films as "Predator," "Lethal Weapon," and "Die Hard," most with equally acclaimed sequels. When he was named Producer of the Year by the National Association of Theatre Owners in 1990, he described Gordon as his "Lieber Meister," echoing Wright's tribute to his own mentor, Louis Sullivan.

Silver has been described as "the soul of the old Hollywood reconstituted in the body—and the exigencies—of the new Hollywood."[6] About him the words "'legend' and 'legendary' come up."[7] He bears striking resemblances to Stevens—not merely in appearance, for Silver, like Stevens, is a large man of commanding presence—but also in the way he works. Like Stevens, he wants to understand all aspects of any activity he supervises. Stuart Baird, one of the film editors who had assisted Silver and whom Silver later made a director, explains it thus:

> Most producers don't intimately understand the process of making a film. He understands it extremely well. He loves the process, he lives the process. He expects his vision to come across: the script, the production design, the sound, the costumes, the music—everything.[8]

Like Stevens, Silver seems always in motion, constantly traveling from one area of operation to another, with sojourns at Auldbrass slotted in whenever possible. And like Stevens, Silver insists on complete control of everything around him, of all aspects of his work, of all moments of his day. "Let's face it," he told an interviewer, "I'm a fanatic about control. I don't even want to *discuss* the notion of losing control. Sleep is enough of a loss of control for me."[9]

Silver's dedication to Wright, demonstrated by his spectacular rescue of two Wright properties, has even brought about a singular union: in what must be a first for *The New York Times*, a review of one of Silver's recent films ("The Matrix") appeared under the signature of the architecture critic. Silver's film, writes Herbert Muschamp, "deserves to be a classic."[10] Muschamp continues,

> It's not a stretch to see parallels between the producer's house and ideas that flicker through his movie. In both the message is freedom from repression symbolized by the ability to move fluidly through space.

While Muschamp refers specifically to Silver's Storer house, in Los Angeles, he could equally well, and perhaps even more

persuasively, have referred to Auldbrass. But the point is well taken. A banner in Muschamp's article proclaims, "That the film's producer is a Frank Lloyd Wright devotee may help explain some of the ideas that flit through it."

Coming into possession of Auldbrass, Silver faced the sort of fundamental questions encountered by all owners of historically significant properties: how to deal with issues of change and continuity, how to determine what degree of intervention would best serve all involved. One extreme option, at best defensible only in academic terms, yet occasionally advocated by preservation purists, would be to do nothing, to stand aside and allow Auldbrass to disintegrate over time, leaving perhaps as its only trace some remnant of a foundation. John Ruskin (1819–1900), who sought in his lifetime to protect ancient monuments against falsified restoration, might have advocated this approach. In his influential writings, which Wright himself admired, he proclaimed,

> I must not leave the truth unstated, that it is again no question of expediency or feeling whether we shall preserve the buildings of past times or not. We have no right whatever to touch them. They are not ours. They belong partly to those who built them, and partly to all the generations of mankind who are to follow us.[11]

While it is difficult to imagine any rational person following such a course with Auldbrass (and even Ruskin offered modifying arguments), once intervention begins, such theoretical purity is subject to compromise. Even the most minimal of acts—arresting the ongoing disintegration of a building such as Auldbrass to stabilize it as a ruin—involves action that might be condemned as arbitrary, for the natural effects of time are altered by human choice, and inevitably materials foreign to the original structure are introduced. To sustain a building in active use rather than retain it as a stabilized ruin inevitably leads to more drastic intervention, and such action necessarily compromises historic purity.

One relatively conservative route toward preservation often taken with historic houses would force the determination of some point in time of particular importance in the history of the plantation. The buildings would then be restored to that time, becoming, in effect, an historic monument, frozen in time. Such a course was taken with Wright's home and studio in Oak Park, where the date of 1909 was selected because that was the last year in which Wright lived in the house and worked in the studio. This necessitated the removal of later alterations by Wright that some considered significant (for he continued to own the property) and required some guesswork in other areas where conditions in 1909 were unclear.[12] If such an approach were taken with Auldbrass, the date selected would proba-

bly be 1962, the year of Stevens's death. In that year, it could be argued, Auldbrass reached its most extensive development by the original client. Yet to take this course (assuming sufficient documentation existed to establish such a framework) would emphasize certain curiosities. For example, it would honor numerous changes made by Stevens's wives that neither he nor Wright supported. This would imply that the human history of the house was as significant as creative genius, and indeed such an interpretation was for a time proposed for the Darwin D. Martin house in Buffalo (1904), where it was argued that closets added by Mrs. Martin should be restored, compromising the spatial openness of the upper story and thus presenting a critical commentary of Wright's design.[13] Whatever the merits of recreating a specific moment in the history of an historic building (and the approach remains debatable), it would fail to yield a fully workable house at Auldbrass.

In other examples, architects reinterpret building elements from earlier generations, integrating historic fragments into new construction so as to enrich the layers of time. Results can be striking, perhaps nowhere better illustrated than in the work of the famous Italian architect, Carlo Scarpa (1906–1978).[14] As described, Scarpa "saw integrity not in the return of a building to some original state but in respect for the gradual accretion of changes that made it 'whole'."[15] Yet in such work ambiguities of historic accuracy can abound. Scarpa's interventions, for example, are characterized as "restoring some elements and adding new ones, integrating the two in a fusion so seamless that the observer is hard pressed to find the juncture between them."[16] Surely such reconfigurations work more effectively in dealing with building accretions of many generations, distant in time and anonymous in nature. How to reconfigure work of the very recent past, work conceived by so towering a genius as Wright, poses more difficult questions. How, for instance, would one select a new architect equal to the task of imposing his (or her) own vision over Wright's?

Another approach to restoration lies at an opposite extreme from Ruskin. Eugène Emmanuel Viollet-le-Duc (1814–1879), Ruskin's nineteenth-century counterpart in the field of preservation, advocated an aggressive approach both in the name of history and in the hope of keeping buildings not as useless ruins, but as active participants in the societies they continued to serve. In certain instances, he believed buildings should even be restored to an idealized state such as might never have existed, for him a necessary corrective for great designs imperfectly realized. As he wrote, "To restore a building is not to preserve it, to repair, or rebuild it; it is to reinstate it in a condition of completeness that could never have existed at any given time."[17] In such instances, the authenticity of original fabric

FIG. 155
MAIN HOUSE
Auldbrass, detail showing decorative
wood panel at top.
Alan Weintraub/Arcaid, 2001

is judged to be of uneven importance, and elements that compromise the attainment of complete artistic integrity, including historic fabric, when judged to be compromised, are sacrificed.

Preservationists in the late twentieth and early twenty-first centuries tend to dismiss Viollet le Duc's approach, although in actual practice it is more often undertaken than is readily acknowledged, and sometimes with very good results indeed.[18] Particularly for buildings of the recent past, where ample documentation records design intentions, and where surviving witnesses can testify as to original conditions, merits can be argued. Even Ruskin made an exception for buildings erected in living memory, believing changes in those examples could be justified.[19] In the case of Auldbrass, which was never completed as originally designed, which was never satisfactorily resolved in the eyes of its client, and which would hold little meaning if left abandoned, the practicality of this approach bears consideration.

Silver soon determined his intentions. Auldbrass was not only to be restored, but to be completed as closely as possible to the way Wright had designed it. Some modifications of that ideal would be required to accommodate changes of function, and to take advantage of newly available materials and technologies, but these were to be as non-intrusive as possible. With the same gift for managing buildings as producing films, Silver then set about assembling the team of experts who would bring these ideas into being. He soon noted parallels with his own profession. "There is a great similarity between architecture and picture making," he observed. "They begin with pure thought and are turned into something that is tangible and can last."[20]

To ensure the greatest possible allegiance to Wright's intentions and to the history of Auldbrass, Silver worked with an ever expanding group of assistants to assemble as complete a set of documents as was possible. Record copies of all drawings, photographs, correspondence, and the like were sought from every possible source: the Frank Lloyd Wright Archives, the Avery Architectural Library at Columbia University, descendants of the original clients, builders, newspaper morgues, anything that might have bearing on the project. These documents he supplemented with interviews and careful examinations of the actual site. Among those making the trip to Auldbrass to assist in this effort was Wesley Peters, Wright's senior apprentice, who had been involved with the construction at the very beginning. Others, too, were asked to recall anything they could about the plantation: how its planning and construction had come about, how it had worked, and how it had been changed. In these ways, work could be undertaken with a minimum of speculation.

With documentary evidence in hand, specific strategies could be developed. These Silver organized according to

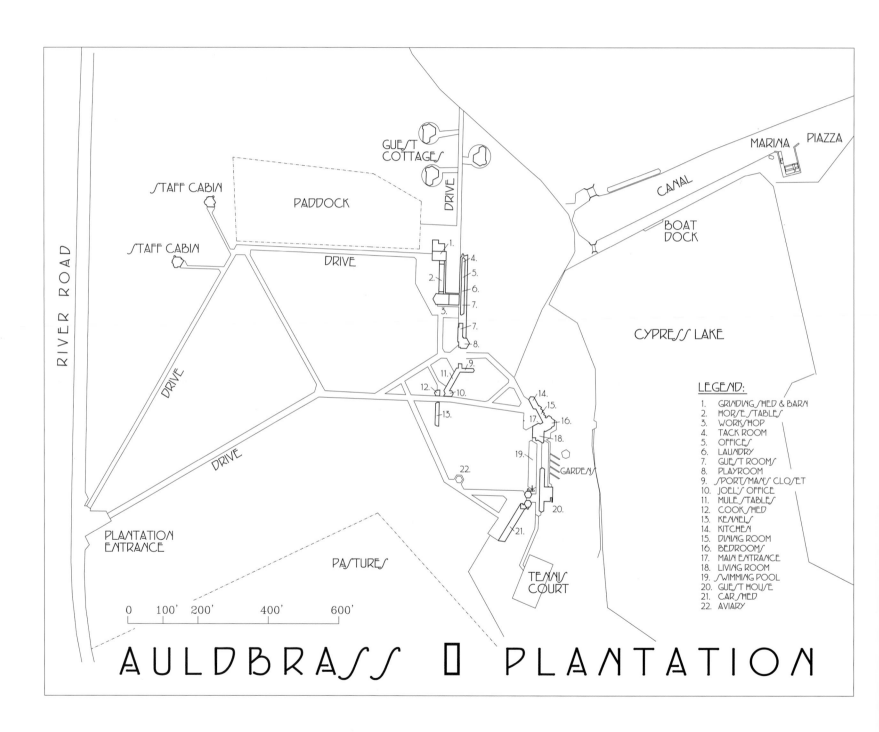

LEGEND:

1. GRINDING SHED & BARN
2. HORSE STABLES
3. WORKSHOP
4. TACK ROOM
5. OFFICES
6. LAUNDRY
7. GUEST ROOMS
8. PLAYROOM
9. SPORTSMAN'S CLOSET
10. JOEL'S OFFICE
11. MULE STABLES
12. COOK SHED
13. KENNELS
14. KITCHEN
15. DINING ROOM
16. BEDROOMS
17. MAIN ENTRANCE
18. LIVING ROOM
19. SWIMMING POOL
20. GUEST HOUSE
21. CAR SHED
22. AVIARY

RIVER ROAD

STAFF CABIN

STAFF CABIN

PADDOCK

GUEST COTTAGES

DRIVE

DRIVE

DRIVE

DRIVE

PLANTATION ENTRANCE

PASTURES

GARDEN

TENNIS COURT

CANAL

BOAT DOCK

MARINA   PIAZZA

CYPRESS LAKE

0   100'   200'   400'   600'

AULDBRASS ☐ PLANTATION

four major phases. First, all of Wright's surviving buildings would be restored as he had originally designed them, retaining as much original fabric as feasible, and, to the degree possible, subtly distinguishing between any new materials and the originals they replaced so as to identify alterations. Second, Wright-designed buildings that had been destroyed or altered beyond recognition would be rebuilt, using materials as close to the originals as possible. Third, Wright's unbuilt projects for the plantation would be realized as he had designed them, adhering to exterior configurations, but with selected interiors reorganized to address current needs. Fourth, new buildings that were needed by Silver would be added, designed for the most part in a manner sympathetic to Wright's scheme, but located at a distance, so they would not intrude.

By 2002, phases one and two had been completed.[21] Phase three was nearing completion with revised working drawings underway for the large guest house—the largest component of this phase remaining. Its construction, together with that of its related dining barge, is scheduled to begin sometime before 2012, and sites were prepared for three additional cottages located in conformance with Wright's aerial perspective of 1940 showing three cabins. Extraneous elements that had remained fragmentary designs, and that had never been specifically located nor fully integrated within Wright's master plan, such as the housekeeper's cottage, were not part of Silver's scheme. Phase four was well advanced, with new buildings located at the periphery of the property, where they created their own ambience, yet in the main sympathetic to Wright's originals.[22]

In evaluating what resulted, the essential, underlying components of Wright's design should be kept in mind. A first essential involves the unity of its parts, the "sameness" of the diverse components established through the consistent use of cypress and copper, and the unity of the whole with its immediate setting, an apparently uncultivated extension of the local terrain. A second essential relates to the angularity of the hexagonal module in plan and section, the means by which the low-profiled, easy, continuous informality of the overall composition and its individual parts are achieved. A third essential deals with permeability, with the screen-like, ventilated quality of the structure achieved through long ranges of glass doors, clerestories, and ventilating panels.

Each of these essential qualities had been compromised. The loss of buildings in the fire had impaired the unity of the composition, as had other additions and changes. These included the substitution of unlined, white gravel driveways for the sharply outlined, darker planes Wright had envisioned; the imposition of Thomas Church's well-meaning but inadequate landscaping plan, more formal in its approach and more obviously cultivated than Wright's design; and

the addition of the small cottage-like kennel by another hand, its diminished form a weak parody of Wright. The sagging roofs and untreated cypress of the original buildings further compromised the unified image essential to Wright's ideal.

Interior changes and additions made by both Stevens and his third wife further compromised the integrity of the angled module. These included the "owners' kitchen" with its discordant vertical walls pushed out under the overhangs and the addition made to the main kitchen. Encumbering window treatments added over the years had impaired the permeability of the walls, as did the unworkable system of ventilating panels.

In his approach, Wright had already identified variables which could form a basis for restoration efforts. First and perhaps most important was his acceptance of the need for change, as stated earlier. In his mind he believed such change to be essential; as he poetically wrote,

> Architecture . . . proceeds, persists, creates according to the nature of man and his circumstances as they both change. . . . The law of organic change is the only thing that mankind can know as beneficent or as actual! We can only know that all things are in process of flowing in some continuous state of becoming.[23]

Pragmatically adhering to this philosophy, Wright had, during the course of design and construction at Auldbrass, continuously modified his plans in recognition of new needs, yet always within the ambit of his modular system. Both unity and angularity could be sustained. Less successfully he had dealt with problems related to permeability. The question of window screens seems never to have been satisfactorily resolved; early suggestions for sunshades (the Aeroshades) and elaborately draped insect screening had given way to more conventional screened panels that reduced the sense of openness. The heavily framed screened enclosure adjoining the caretaker's house had proven difficult to maintain and had long since been removed. Most of the ventilating panels along the bases and tops of exterior walls would no longer open. Further unresolved was the question of air conditioning, for while the house was comfortable enough during much of the year, it was not so at the height of summer, a time when it had originally been assumed that few except a presumably resilient staff would be in residence.

Silver remained in command of each of these issues as they were addressed by the architects and consultants he assembled. As restoration architect, following early discussions, he selected Eric Lloyd Wright, Wright's grandson. As noted, Eric had already worked with Silver on the restoration of the Storer house, and he brought the undeniable dis-

ABOVE
FIG. 157
**RECONSTRUCTION
OF ROOF**

Auldbrass, main house. Courtesy Joel Silver,
1989

RIGHT
FIG. 158
**POLISHING FLOOR OF NEW
DINING ROOM ENCLOSURE**

Auldbrass, main house. Blaine Waller; courtesy
Joel Silver

FIG. 159
**ENCLOSED PASSAGE
IN MAIN HOUSE**
Auldbrass, looking through windows to
front door. Alan Weintraub/Arcaid, 2001

FOLLOWING PAGES
FIG. 160
**DINING ROOM ENCLOSURE,
MAIN HOUSE**
Auldbrass, with tables separated. Anthony
Peres, 2001

tinction of being an immediate descendant of the great man. Silver praises his interpretation of the documentary evidence that had been carefully assembled but required critical evaluation.[24]

Eric Lloyd Wright, in turn, identified an architect working in the area who could serve as site supervisor: Ben Strahan, who had studied at Taliesin and who then maintained an office on Hilton Head Island, not far from Auldbrass. Strahan, however, was to be involved only during the early stages of the project, during the first and much of the second phases, before relocating to Nashville. Silver then decided that he and Eric could better undertake this responsibility themselves, relying for local assistance on another architect with an office in Hilton Head Island: Tom Crews, who had earlier worked for Strahan and been involved with Auldbrass while at that office.

During the summer of 1987, the conditions of the existing buildings were assessed and all assembled documents studied. Work on the main house began that fall and continued for two years.[25] All elements inimical to Wright's

design were removed, most obviously the "owners' kitchen" added by Nina Lunn Stevens and the extension of the main kitchen, but also the aluminum-painted built-up roofing (by then a shapeless mass) and the conventional downspouts. The house itself was taken back to its essentials: painted surfaces stripped, derelict plumbing and kitchen fixtures removed, decayed remnants of the interior sliding insect screens removed (and stored elsewhere on the site).

Rebuilding proved to be ambitious, but remained sympathetic to Wright's original intent (fig. 3, see pp. 6-7). The concrete floors, their continuous, unbroken surfaces so vital a component of his design, were made level, with sunken and cracked portions replaced. Immediately the problem of heating became acute, for resuscitating the system of radiant pipes buried within the floor would have been impossible without reconstructing the entire concrete slab, which would have required the disassembly of the house itself and needless destruction of other portions of the concrete slab, for major areas of the floor remained in good shape. Instead, a new mechanical system was added, threaded

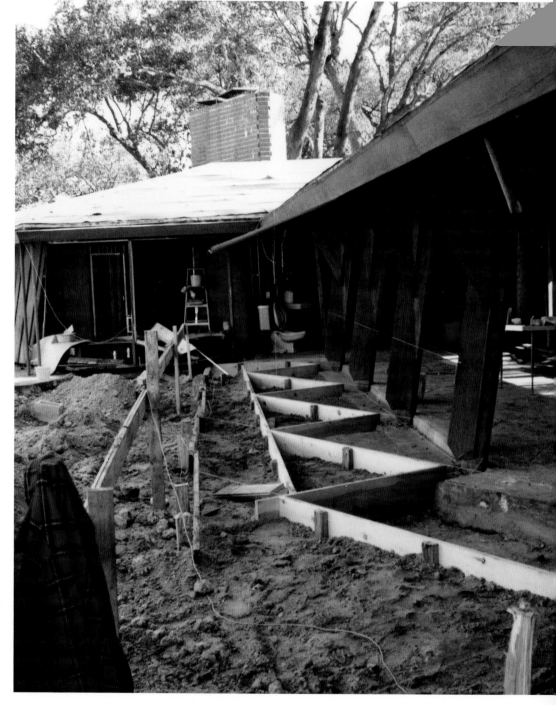

carefully through and around historic elements so that it remained nearly invisible.

Consulting engineers determined that a heat pump would offer the most efficient means of both heating and cooling (for Silver had early determined that cooling would be essential to his needs). This meant drilling a series of deep wells around the perimeter of the buildings, each well going down to a depth of around 200 feet to supply water for a closed loop that would provide the transfer medium. Because such well water maintains a constant temperature, neither too cold nor too hot, it could be "pumped" for both heating and cooling.

In the house, the largest pieces of mechanical equipment for the heating and cooling systems were neatly concealed by locating them behind the living room fireplace.[26] Yet replacing the radiant heating by a hot-air system implied that a system of ducts be added to move the heated (and, additionally, cooled) air. This in a building without any attic or basement, without even crevices within walls or above ceilings. The solution required long, painstaking effort.

Concurrent restoration work on the fireplaces aided efforts in at least one instance. Because these fireplaces had been partly closed in an effort to improve their draft, Silver ordered that they be re-opened to be in accord with Wright's original design. In studying the living room fireplace in preparation for this work, bricked-in openings above the hearth that Wright had designed as apertures for speakers were discovered. They could be (and were) reopened to serve as supply grills for that major space (fig. 150). At the same time, the clerestory in the living room was restored to its original appearance of alternating wood and glass panels, a pattern that enhanced its presence as a decorative band; Nina had substituted glass for wood so it was entirely glazed and less subtle. Elsewhere, relatively small pipes carrying heated or chilled liquid took the place of conventional ducts. Again, other work facilitated their location. To make horizontal alignment of the extended eaves a reality, steel plates were being added along a few major beams, notably in the living room and the smaller bedroom. Wood panels, kept thin to minimize added thickness, were to be affixed to conceal the steel. Within these reinforced beams, which were centrally located, the pipes, too, could be hidden. They led to fan units that would supply the heated or cooled air, and these were carefully located over built-in wardrobes or behind storage units, so that again the added elements remained essentially invisible.

Throughout the plantation, the extent of mechanical improvements reflected new demands. Following the fire of 1952, electric lines had been brought in above ground; they were now relocated below ground, where they were out of sight, as Wright had originally planned. Silver bought a trencher to facilitate the digging of needed ditches, for in addition to increased electric service, he also required a gas line, underground irrigation pipes for the managed landscape, satellite connections for television and a sophisticated telephone system. Like the new system for heating and cooling, all is hidden. Yet beneath the seemingly untouched terrain lie nearly 6,000 linear feet of hidden cables and pipes.

Turning to what initially seemed to be simpler issues led to yet further complication. When Silver first contemplated buying Auldbrass, he had assured himself that its restoration would be an easier task than the Storer house had been, for surely the repair of wood construction was far simpler than the repair of Wright's experimental concrete blocks. In actuality the reverse proved true, and the unpre-

FIG. 162
DINING ROOM ENCLOSURE
Auldbrass, with tables joined and main gateway through farm buildings visible in distance. Anthony Peres, 2001

dictably complicated angles that had so frustrated Stevens and his builders also frustrated Silver and his.[27]

Although most of the original cypress appeared to be salvageable, some was quite obviously beyond saving, and elsewhere, the removal of unsympathetic additions would require sensitive repair. Clearly a carpenter with special skills was required, preferably someone who had worked on Wright's buildings before. As Silver relates, his first lead in identifying this carpenter came from a symposium on the conservation of Wright buildings that he attended in March 1988,[28] when a young apprentice carpenter who had worked on the restoration of the first Herbert Jacobs house (Madison, Wisconsin, 1937) introduced himself. Silver now sought him out, convincing him to move to Auldbrass and undertake the work at hand. A student from Clemson University who had taken up temporary residence in the main house (as a guard against further disintegration) was to serve as his assistant.

The apprentice carpenter began work on the cook shed, partly to learn a bit about the complexities of the structural system before beginning on the main house, and partly to render a more habitable place for his own camp. After disassembling the small structure to study its parts, he found himself unable to put it together again, and its parts sat forlornly on the lawn like some wooden Humpty-Dumpty after the fall. In understandable desperation he called on a more experienced carpenter for help: Kendall Pierce, who had been the lead carpenter at the Jacobs house. Pierce came and soon demonstrated his remarkable skills. Silver is effusive in his praise, referring to Pierce's arrival as a turning point in the project. "Kendall could follow the grammar," Silver says; the myriad angles, the complicated intersections, the delicacy of retrofitting—all were handled with superb result, yet with seeming ease."[29]

Yet it must have been far from easy. A typical component of a door frame, for example, required twenty complicated cuts; Pierce devised jigs to facilitate such work. During the course of rebuilding the main house, doors were reglazed and repaired, as were the insect screens which Silver wanted to retain in the two bedrooms. In the main living space, where during summer days air conditioning would prevail, the disintegrating screens that had been removed were placed in storage, available for future use should they be wanted. Meanwhile their removal allowed the openness of the glass doors to be experienced without an intervening layer.

Selected examples of the ventilating panels that ran along the bottom and top of exterior walls were restored to an operable condition as a record of the original design; others were left in place, but sealed. Where the "owners' kitchen" had so awkwardly abutted, with walls pushed out under the overhanging eaves to capture additional space there and in the adjacent dining alcove, the original profiles were rebuilt.

Pierce, having fully won Silver's trust, remained in charge of the carpentry until the Wright buildings were restored and the missing Wright buildings rebuilt. Just before work was fully complete he received another emergency call—help was needed with the restoration of Wright's Loren Pope house (Falls Church, Virginia, 1940). With Silver's grateful praise he journeyed on to reassemble yet another example of Wright's design, leaving details at Auldbrass to his associates. Silver, who mourns Pierce's subsequent death, describes Auldbrass as "not carpentry, but cabinetry . . . without Kendall it couldn't have happened as it is."[30] His work has been continued by another carpenter, Rick Wrightman, who has been responsible for new additions such as the river pavilion and guest cottages (see Epilogue).

Complicating the issue of carpentry was the wood itself. Much of the original Tidewater Red Cypress was indeed salvageable, for while seriously discolored, it had proved to be as resistant to decay as its original specifications had promised. Yet a certain amount of new wood was needed to replace those parts that had not survived, and none was available. Refusing to accept this seeming fact, Silver began to search on his own, and through a lumber baron that he located, discovered an unexpected source: a used wine vat in Michigan. Disassembled, its staves provided the needed replacements for the main house and surviving farm buildings. More was needed to replace those buildings that had been lost in the fire of 1952, but in those locations Silver wisely used the more readily available white cypress, dyed to match the red. This effects a sensible differentiation, for through examination future conservators can clearly distinguish the original buildings from those that were replaced.

No sooner did Silver and his assistants solve one problem, it seems, then another arose. Thus with the carpentry under control, the next question became one of protective finish, for it was critical to recapture the original honey-brown color of the exposed wood that Wright and Stevens had worked so steadfastly to achieve. Determined to find the best finish possible, Silver considered a variety of options, settling at last on a marine oil imported from Finland and sold under the brand name Deks-ojle.[31] Randall Mackinson, then curator of the Gamble house in Pasadena, California, had recommended the product, for it had proved excellent in the maintenance of that remarkable wood structure of 1908 by Greene and Greene. Silver also applied it to redwood surfaces in the Storer house.

The gray, discolored boards of Auldbrass were thus sanded and refinished with Deks-ojle, which is more usually used on boats. Miraculously, the original color that people recalled was regained (fig. 56). Yet to maintain this color

requires the same ongoing reapplications as had the less ideal liquid creosote: annually for the exterior walls, alternate years for the exterior soffits, and once a decade inside.

For the first application of the Deks-ojle, Silver and Pierce had realized that no ordinary painters could do the job required, as staining such complicated buildings to exacting specifications would be far from routine. Pierce's wife, Pamela, who had supervised the staining of the Jacobs house, agreed to undertake this new and more demanding task. She journeyed to Auldbrass and assembled a small team of local painters, whom she trained. It takes that team of eight or nine people around two weeks to stain the exteriors of the buildings and the expansive fences.[32]

Problems of finish also arose with the exposed red concrete floors throughout the plantation, for the old ones were very much in need of work and the new ones had no finish at all. Wright had wanted them waxed so they glowed softly like old leather. Again, finding the right material proved difficult, for the original wax was no longer available. Seeking owners of other Wright properties with similarly exposed floors, Silver was led to Roy Palmer, then owner of the Wright house in Greenville, South Carolina known as Broad Margin (1951), originally designed for Charles and Gabrielle Austin. Palmer gave Silver a can of the wax that he found stored in the house, but it came with no hint of how it should be applied and turned the floors of Auldbrass into what Silver describes as a "gummy mess that got progressively worse."[33]

In his pursuit of a better solution, Silver was next led to the renowned but hardly Wrightian architect, Michael Graves. Graves was working on a house in Malibu owned by a friend of Silver's and referred Silver to Steve Guild, an acquaintance of Graves from New Jersey. Guild, in turn, located the descendant firm of the original manufacturer of the magic wax.[34] Because that wax had a petroleum base and could no longer meet legal restrictions for manufacture, it could not be reproduced, but the company developed a similar wax with a water base. This time the wax came with instructions to guide its application.[35]

Even with instructions, application of the wax proved difficult. Following discussion of the method to be employed, Guild perfected the system, one not unlike that once used by military personnel to shine shoes. It is essentially a heat process, with wax applied to burlap which in turn is attached to a buffer. With buffing the burlap warms and the wax melts as it is applied (fig. 158). It took days to strip the floors of their earlier layers of wax in preparation for this process, but ultimately the desired finish was achieved, one easily maintained by dry buffing, with stunning results. Unlike the petroleum-base wax, the water-base wax whitens

if spotted by water, but can be repaired, Silver recounts, by rubbing the surface with burlap moistened with a small amount of liquid wax .

Silver's determination to achieve the ideal affected even the roofing of the complex. There had been no question of removing the amorphous layers of built-up roofing and aluminum paint that Wright had so hated, and copper of the sort Wright had originally wanted was readily available. Yet there was no exact specification of what gauge copper Wright would have specified, for before that decision was reached he had agreed to substitute the copper foil that had performed so miserably. As Wright himself might have wanted had the budget allowed, Silver elected to use a luxuriously thick sheeting (20-gauge) rather than the thinner sheeting (16-gauge) more commonly used; this would provide an extra guard against the acid-bearing leaves that fell in such profusion each year.

A significant amount of copper was required. Although work began with the main house, once the other buildings and linking connections on the plantation were similarly roofed (including those newly rebuilt), a total floor area of 17,000 square feet would need to be covered. Silver explains how Thomas Schmidt again offered assistance, drawing on personal connections to contact Universal Roofing of Pittsburgh and helping secure a good price for the needed material; it was installed according to the exacting standards demanded by the design. The main house was the first to be completed (fig. 157), yet when finished the bent angle of the copper panels appeared lower than Wright's elevation drawings. The higher angle used for the other buildings achieved the desired effect, and Silver, ever seeking perfection, plans to rebuild the roof of the main house to conform.

Copper was also required for the downspouts that Wright had designed, but that had never been realized. Again there was no question in Silver's mind, nor in others connected with the work, that these were essential to the completed vision of Auldbrass. The decorative wood pendants that Wright had designed as a substitute worked visually, but could not carry water, which had necessitated the further additions of conventional downspouts at each corner, and these so closely resembled columns that all sense of the elegant cantilevers was lost, as noted earlier. Whatever the degree of compromise, the decorative pendants had been designed by Wright, so they were carefully removed and saved. Yet once the more finely detailed, working copper downspouts were installed, the greater quality of the first design became apparent, and together with other exterior improvements, the house could at last begin to be seen as Wright had depicted it in his drawings (fig. 6).

Inside the main house, the complicated history of earlier plan adjustments was exploited to arrive at a more workable arrangement. The master bathrooms, which Stevens had subjected to seemingly continuous modifications, were now rearranged again within their outlined shapes, but more sensitively to the underlying hexagonal module.[36] The smaller bedroom had been more radically modified to suit Nina's wishes; wanting more space, she had contrived to have one wall pushed out beneath the eaves, and this had adverse effects: it compromised the continuity of the broad overhangs, the exterior surface of the relocated wall itself weathered badly without its roofed protection, and the beams above, now made to span a greater distance to that relocated wall, sagged over time. The wall was pulled back to its original location and the sagging beams were made straight (fig. 100), but Silver remains less than fully satisfied, for his study of the design drawings shows that Wright had indeed wanted the eaves extended still further.[37] Whether that would also have led to sagging beams has so far remained unanswered.

Nina had also expanded the living room terrace to form a continuous concrete band around the entire perimeter of the house. Her need, she claimed, had been to provide an easy route for a wheeled log carrier, so that it might more readily service the various fireplaces. Silver left that portion of her expanded terrace outside the two bedrooms, where it proved an agreeable feature, but along the lakeside elevation of the kitchen and the side of the living area facing the parking court, these paved extensions added an unwanted visual interruption to the continuity of the inclined walls with their setting, and Silver had them removed (fig. 45). Two log carts, somewhat awkward, top-heavy contraptions that Stevens designed with the idea of relating them to the grammar of the house and had fabricated by his Muskegon Boiler Works, had been sold by the Lorings along with the Wright-designed furniture. The single duplicate now at Auldbrass was also made by the same Works. But the cart is no longer critical to servicing the fireplaces, as most have been fitted for gas flames. This was done partly to lessen the danger of another conflagration, but mostly to prevent them from smoking, for Wright tended to design fireplaces with monumental openings that exceeded the capacity of the flue to draw. This was why Nina had

modified the livingroom fireplace opening in the first place, by raising its hearth to bring about a better ratio between the area of the opening and its flue; Silver believed the original design more important, whatever its flaws. Eric Lloyd Wright based his design for the gas flames on one frequently used by his father, Lloyd Wright: lava rocks are mounded over a gas pipe buried within, placed to draw up the fire in a picturesque manner.

The main kitchen's extension that Stevens had added was removed, and the porch that Wright had intended restored, yet with a refinement of its base. When fully opened with only insect screening as a visual barrier, a stair that led down to a food storage area below, and its attendant pipe railing, were unflatteringly revealed. To create a more agreeable juxtaposition, Eric Lloyd Wright adapted the porch wall of the staff cabin, which is screened above but incorporates a low wood-paneled base below, and which is opened at the very base by a narrow band of screen to facilitate ventilation (fig. 149).

Once the smaller, original configuration of the kitchen was recaptured, interior modifications made by Stevens became even more unworkable, and they were removed. Wright had shown the stove at the center with a ventilator

FIG. 169
DRESSING AREA ADJOINING SMALL BEDROOM
Auldbrass, main house. Alan Weintraub/ Arcaid, 2001

planned above; Stevens had relocated the stove, and the ventilator was never built. New appliances and countertops have been added to render the kitchen more workable than it had probably ever been, with an island counter at the center rather than the stove, and a cupola has been built above to honor the exterior profile that Wright planned.

The covered passage linking the kitchen to the main house was at last enclosed as Wright had indicated in his revision of 1953 (fig. 161), and the front door relocated as he had suggested, so that it lay outside this newly enclosed space (fig. 159).[38] It proved to be a complicated essay in joinery, for to achieve the elaborately angled glass required that the individual panes be mitred on each side, and for the glass panes to fit smoothly into the wood stanchions required exactingly crafted slots. Yet these seemingly minor details are critical to Wright's work, for they facilitate the seamless continuity of space that he had long championed, and that Silver had come so fully to appreciate. Also according to Wright's planned revision of 1953, yet another fireplace was added to the ten already existing at the plantation (fig. 160). The raised hearth facing the dining area serves as an open cooking grill, in this instance its opening correctly proportioned so that it does not smoke, and the chimney rising above adds a firm vertical accent.

The study, no longer wanted as a dining space, was restored as originally conceived by Wright, and the adjacent covered passage that would one day link the main house to the future guest house was rebuilt, an extension of the house on the opposite side of the kitchen porch and one essential to the full composition.

Under Eric Lloyd Wright's supervision, new furniture, both built-in and freestanding, was fabricated according to his grandfather's original drawings. As in the reconstruction of the missing buildings, no lost skills or forgotten techniques were required to bring them into being, and sufficient red cypress was available so that they could be built in the material originally planned. In the same spirit, additional modular tables and chairs like those in the main living area that Wright had also planned to use in the new dining area were at last built (fig. 162).[39] As with the identical tables and chairs of the main living area which Wright had earlier specified, they allow a flexibility of use that helps energize the space.

In his furniture layouts, Wright had indicated lounge chairs that were never built and that Silver now wanted to realize. In plan the chair seemed similar to one built for the Friedman house, and Silver was prepared to authorize its use as a model. Then drawings and a model of the chair designed specifically for Auldbrass were discovered with Stevens's prints of the working drawings that his daughter had deposited in the Avery Architectural Library. Three examples of this elegant design were fabricated, and those fortunate enough to recline in their welcoming cushions come to realize that Wright could indeed design seating of great comfort (fig. 166).[40]

The plan of Wright's angular beds had proved frustrating to the original supplier of bed linens, as earlier noted. They apparently proved frustrating to Stevens as well, for he had realized them as conventional rectangles, then added triangular hassocks at one end to complete Wright's intended profile. In replacing these pieces, Silver had them made according to Wright's original scheme. In the time that had elapsed since they were first designed, unusual shapes for beds seemed somehow less extreme to a gener-

ation more used to personal luxury, and custom linens were made without wondering questions.

The system of suspended light sconces that Wright specified had been fabricated and installed for Stevens, but they were stolen while the furnishings were in storage.[41] They had been designed in two lengths (the longer for use over the beds), to be made of strap metal with conical green shades that rested directly on the bulbs, and they were detailed to slide along a track of continuous plug molds at the perimeter of the house, providing a flexible system that anticipated later methods of track lighting. One surviving example was discovered during the early stages of work, confirming their detailing, and a full set was reproduced for the house (fig. 137). At some point they had been supplemented by fluorescent tubes concealed behind fascia boards bordering the ceilings; the additional light they cast down adjoining wall surfaces would have been welcome had it not been so glaring. The fluorescent tubes were replaced by a product not available in Wright's time: tube incandescents with filaments casting light of a softer color that can also be dimmed. Thus the basic shape of the older tubes are retained, but they produce light of a more sympathetic color and of variable intensity.[42]

These same lights were installed in some outlying buildings of the plantation, all of which were restored in the same spirit, and with a similar care, as the main house. The caretaker's house posed the most severe problems. During the fire of 1952, water had eroded the ground beneath its con-

LEFT
FIG. 173
GUN ROOM (NOW OFFICE)
Auldbrass. Anthony Peres, 2010

RIGHT
FIG. 174
GUN ROOM (NOW OFFICE)
Auldbrass. Anthony Peres, 2010

crete slab, causing part of the floor to drop. Much of the area beneath the house had to be further excavated, the floor raised on jacks to its original position, and the area backfilled to secure the needed stability.

The plan of the caretaker's house had always been problematic. It had been narrowed by one modular unit after construction had begun, probably to pull further back from a drainage stream along the building's outer side. On the drawings showing its larger dimension, a linear shelf unit extending from the fireplace defined a passage leading from the entry to the bedrooms beyond. The passage was built with this defining element, but with the reduction in the building's width it left barely room to pass. As in Wright's other space-conserving Usonian houses, space allocated to such corridors was minimal, and here perhaps too much so, for its two-foot dimension was measured at the bottom rather than the top of the inwardly-inclined walls. This unit had been removed and sold at auction before Silver acquired the property. To reinsert it would have necessitated widening the building, obviously too radical a modification. But the bare wall and undefined passage were not ideal as left. So narrow shelves were added along the outer wall, providing needed storage and suggesting the presence of the unit that had once been planned (see fig. 83).

As in the main house, various other changes had been made to the caretaker's house over the years that Stevens occupied Auldbrass. To adapt it for her guests, Nina had added a low window and a pair of doors where the original kitchen had once been. The low window was removed so the kitchen could be rebuilt to serve the newly refur-

bished living area, but the doors were left to provide access to the adjoining terrace. Added to the space was a large projection screen for the entertainment of Silver's guests, but it rolls away into a concealed slot in the ceiling. Nina had removed the built-in bunk beds in the two children's bedrooms, believing them too small for her guests, but Silver thought otherwise, and they have been rebuilt.

The kennels were restored to their original use, but with fewer dogs housed there than Stevens had originally planned. There was no need, then, for the adjacent pens, which had become unsightly fenced enclosures, and they were removed. The nearby cook shed seems never to have been used as originally planned, but rather had been modified from the start as an additional sleeping cabin. During her years at Auldbrass, Nina grandly referred to it as the gate house, but it never really served that purpose, either. It continues in use as a sleeping cabin, now for guests, but with Nina's unnecessary changes removed.

Stevens's saddle and gun room, complete with its own fireplace, had originally held gun racks as well as a locked liquor cabinet of impressive dimensions, and in the tradition of the South the room had served as a place of private, male-dominated conviviality. Stevens later used it as his office, as does Silver, and for that it works very well indeed, overlooking both the main house and the approach from the outer gate. Yet the bigger bath that Nina added so it might also serve for guests was removed, and smaller facilities as shown on the original plans rebuilt.

The adjacent stables for horses were small, and with low roofs, sized for small horses known as Marsh Tackies that

RIGHT
FIG. 175
STAFF CABIN
Auldbrass. Alan Weintraub/Arcaid, 2001

LEFT
FIG. 176
INTERIOR OF STAFF CABIN
Auldbrass, with main room at left and porch at right joined by canvas-covered doors.
Anthony Peres, 2001

OPPOSITE
FIG. 177
SCREENED PORCH
Auldbrass, staff cabin. Alan Weintraub/Arcaid, 2001

are specific to the area. Except for some steel plates added to the stanchions to prevent the animals from chewing the wood, no changes were made (fig. 73). At the end of the enclosure, adjacent to these stables, Wright had incorporated a small building for the storage of hay. Nina had altered it slightly by closing its ventilating walls and outfitting it with a cedar closet for storage; that closet has been removed, and it now serves as a storage facility for the main house. Across the way was an enclosure with bins for the storage of feed; with the addition of built-in table and bench, it is now Silver's gun safe.

Both staff cabins, which had fallen into a sorry state of dilapidation, were rebuilt (figs. 175, 178). In each, the layout of the main room with its cooking area along one side was retained, as was the enclosed screen porch along the two angled walls at the front, but the privy at the back corner was removed, and the small sleeping nook just inside converted to a bath, to better house residents. According to Silver's estate manager, when used for guests, they were the most sought-after accommodations.[43] For Wright had made the staff cabins one of the most appealing features of the estate; they seem to capture the very essence of his full concept, with a focused, angled intensity that clearly states the plantation's underlying themes.[44] As so often in Wright's work, he gave special attention to enhancing what might otherwise have been a lowly place.

Buildings destroyed in the fire of 1952 were rebuilt over their surviving foundations by following the original working drawings, something Stevens had wanted to do, but could not afford (figs. 74, 179, 181). In the first of two minor departures, the roof of the original cow shed was raised slightly to allow adequate head room for full-sized horses,[45] yet the alteration is not readily visible. Thus the continuous line of angled roofs originally housing the machine shed, cow shed, chicken coops, and laundry was effectively regained (fig. 180).

In the second departure, the long, narrow building originally housing the chicken coops, dairy, laundry, and additional storage was widened slightly toward the lake when rebuilt so that it might better serve other needs, for Silver had no desire to raise chickens or operate a dairy, and with modern equipment the laundry could be more efficiently contained. The change is barely detectable. Different uses have been assigned to this enclosure, including a new saddle room at the far end, across from the original cow shed now used to stable horses (fig. 156). Also located in the widened building are a small laundry, caretaker's office, and two additional guest rooms. And near the center, next to the manager's office, is an archive containing copies of all surviving documents of the original plantation and its rebuilding, a welcome resource for the study of Wright's design. Traces of the original chicken yards were removed.

FIG. 178
INTERIOR DURING RESTORATION
Auldbrass, staff cabin. Courtesy Joel Silver, 1988

Except for reinforcing its beams, no changes were made to the machine shed and adjacent shop when rebuilt, and each serves its original purpose. Included among the implements and vehicles kept in the shed are small sports vehicles and more than eight golf carts (painted Cherokee red) to ease travel about the plantation for Silver, his family, staff, and guests. The newly equipped shop serves as a major work area for plantation needs; many of the rebuilt cabinets were, in fact, constructed there. The large barn with the taller roof at the far end of the outlying buildings was also rebuilt without change.

The construction of elements originally conceived for Auldbrass, but never built, brings the design to that state of completion such as never existed before. As realized, they amplify essential qualities of the overall composition. Perhaps most important to Wright was the freestanding pavilion that worked as a pivot, at first identified as an aviary,

then later a tea pavilion and even a housekeeper's cottage. It now stands as Wright first envisioned, an open, screened enclosure housing exotic birds (fig. 183). Two additional elements were proposed by Wright as he continuously added to his design. The first was a small, low grinding shed (for grain) to be attached to the far end of the hay barn, away from the other buildings. Wright positioned it so it would effectively terminate the long composition, and as built it now serves the larger visual function he intended, reintroducing the lower roof line of the farm buildings so the taller barn is more effectively contained (fig. 180). Also constructed according to Wright's detailed drawings are the main gate and adjacent fencing along the county road, elegantly framing the first views to the plantation and visually extending its grammar to the far edge of the property. (fig. 146)

Extending the line of the main house and reinforcing the roofed link between that building and the guest house was

ABOVE
FIG. 179
**RECONSTRUCTION OF
FARM BUILDINGS LOST IN FIRE**
Auldbrass. Courtesy Joel Silver

RIGHT
FIG. 180
FARM BUILDINGS
Auldbrass, with grinding shed and barn at left.
Anthony Peres, 2002

to be a long, narrow, hexagonal swimming pool that Wright had envisioned, its sides sloped elegantly outward from top to bottom. This device not only mirrors the sloped walls of the buildings, but also adds to the apparent depth of the water, suggesting indefinite enclosure. As completed (figs. 188, 189, 190, 191),[46] it invitingly awaits the addition of a final component: the main guest house. Eric Lloyd Wright has prepared drawings that show this element detailed with great care.[47] In this instance, the external profile of Wright's original design has been carefully replicated, but internal arrangements have been modified to better accommodate Silver's needs (fig. 193). Thus the main living spaces and adjoining terraces will be realized as Wright envisioned, but the long ranges of small bedrooms will be replaced by a reduced number of more luxurious and more private accommodations, and facilities for hunters will be reconfigured to be more in accord with the recreational needs of Silver's family. Silver even plans to

build the floating dining barge, having configured the edge of the nearby bank to bring the guest house and its attached pier within its ambit, a feat Wright never quite managed.

In Wright's aerial perspective of Auldbrass, three cabins were shown at the top of the sheet, extending the line of the farm buildings into the distant wetlands (see fig. 23). By the time Stevens and Wright had resolved their differences over the site plan, Stevens had evidently decided to stop with the two that were built, and to locate them closer to the main road. But the appeal of that perspective has remained strong to Silver, and he plans to add those three in the positions Wright first indicated. The sites for the three have been cleared and raised foundation pads prepared.

As work on the main house and related outbuildings progressed, Silver and Eric Lloyd Wright addressed issues related to other components of the site. The unfinished cottage beyond the kitchen (in large part, for Nina's dogs) and hexagonal tool shed, further away, were clearly at odds

with Wright's conception, and both were removed. So, too, were the rigid hexagonal garden wall and equally inflexible planting beds of Church's insensitive landscaping plan, for he had mistakenly interpreted Wright's hexagonal module as a design element in itself rather than a system used to compose a more complicated, interrelated whole. In their place, Wright's design of a low brick wall to partly enclose the parking court (see fig. 120) and a low planter near the bedrooms was realized.

Throughout the grounds, native plants of the sort Wright had originally specified were planted. Along the back of the farm buildings, away from the main house, these are massed along an open channel that functions partly for storm drainage, but that Wright designed in the spirit of a water garden. Wright had also indicated masses of azaleas near the buildings, in beds shaped in accord with his approach to plantings in other locations.[48] As now added they form that same intermediate, clarifying band between seemingly uncultivated land and the more formal shapes of the buildings themselves (fig. 120).

What might seem uncultivated to the unknowing eye actually reflects considerable effort: vast expanses of ground beneath native trees have been both sodded and planted to create some forty acres of managed grounds that conform in appearance to Wright's drawings (fig. 38). It takes a team of mowers one day to cut the grass, and it is cut at sixty-degree angles rather than in more efficient circular motions. For Silver, this special adherence to Wright's hexagonal module justifies the effort.

Creating the expansive lake that both Wright and Stevens had wanted, and that Stevens had at least briefly achieved, required still more effort. More than 3,000 trees had to be cleared from the swampy remains of the earlier attempt at its construction, and other nearby stands of trees were thinned to create desired vistas (title page). And as Stevens had known all too well, powerful

OPPOSITE
FIG.186
VIEW TOWARD FARM BUILDINGS
Auldbrass, with aviary at far right.
Paul Rocheleau, 2003

ABOVE
FIG. 184
**REPRODUCTION OF
A LIGHTING STANDARD**

The sculpture is a reproduction of a
lighting standard designed by Alfonzo
Iannelli for Wright's Midway Gardens
in Chicago, which stood from 1913 to
1929. Paul Rocheleau, 2003

RIGHT
FIG. 185
RUSTIC LANTERN

The rustic stone lantern was orignally in
Japan's old capitol, Kyoto. Paul Rocheleau,
2003

FIG. 187
**GRINDING SHED
(AT FAR LEFT) AND BARN**
Auldbrass. Anthony Peres, 2010

pumps were needed to keep the lake filled. All has been done, and this time the pumps are kept in working order. They not only keep the restored lake filled with water from the river, but can also be used to maintain water levels in a new duck pond and supply water for irrigating the expansive gardens.

Always essential to Wright's vision were the linear, angled roadways that joined his vast complex into a single composition. They had been partly realized, yet without the swale he envisioned as forming a distinct, but flush, edge. And as earlier noted, white gravel had been used rather than the red he had specified. With some difficulty, Silver managed to locate the source of a suitable ruby red granite gravel (in Wisconsin, as he remembers). But to transport it to the site would have added enormously to its cost. Instead, Silver and Eric Lloyd Wright settled for the same color in crushed brick, obtainable from a much closer source in North Carolina and more economical to ship. Yet because crushed brick is less stable than the gravel—it tends to move more easily, and to powder—the swales Wright had designed would not contain it neatly; in fact, it is doubtful if they would have contained the harder gravel neatly, either. Low curbings were substituted so that the clear linear definition Wright depicted in his drawings would prevail (fig. 76).[49]

Silver has gradually acquired land adjacent to his original holdings, regaining more of the expansive acreage of Auldbrass. New roads lead through areas surrounding the lake and along the river, but these roads are edged with metal rather than low curbings, helping to distinguish them from the original layout. Within these annexed areas, and not visible from the historic core of the plantation, are new elements that Silver added as part of his fourth phase of work. Four have so far been designed by Eric Lloyd Wright in sympathy with his grandfather's designs. River House, the first to be completed (in 1996), is an appealingly isolated, hexagonal pavilion on the banks of the river, sited so it expands the parameters of the original plantation (fig. 195). Two copper-roofed pavilions that house pumping equipment to supply water for the lake (as well as related uses) were finished in 1997, and a marina for boats was completed by 2002 (fig. 198).

In another, more isolated corner of the estate, Silver has erected a prefabricated storage building to house damaged pieces removed from the house, but not reused, such as decayed doors and screen panels. In a way, it is another sort of archive. He also uses it as a depot for things that might be needed in the future, such as a cache of Crane plumbing fixtures conforming to Wright's original specifications; these Silver buys from salvage shops to ensure a ready supply of replacements. A car barn has also been added in a remote location. It contains two quite extraordinary automobiles acquired by Silver: Frank Lloyd Wright's own customized Lincoln Continentals, a 1940 Cabriolet (which Wright had significantly reconfigured) and a 1941 Coupe. Both have been restored to running

ABOVE
FIG. 190
DETAIL OF SWIMMING POOL
Auldbrass. Anthony Peres, 2010

RIGHT
FIG. 191
SWIMMING POOL
Auldbrass, with main house terrace at left.
Anthony Peres, 2010

FOLLOWING PAGES
FIG. 192
**MAIN HOUSE WITH
LAKE ON RIGHT**
Auldbrass.
Paul Rocheleau, 2003

condition under Silver's direction and completed right down to their color: Wright's signature Cherokee red.[50]

More than 500 newly installed outdoor lights create appealing ambience at night. Small and well-placed, they remain largely unnoticed during the day, but at night illuminate the vast expanses of lawn and tall trees. Eric Lloyd Wright helped with their selection, and he included some of his own design that he had earlier developed for his father's Wayfarers' Chapel (Palos Verdes, California, 1946). They relate effectively to the original buildings. Gary Skewes, a lighting consultant from Florida, identified from work published in *House and Garden*, determined their numbers and locations to ensure, as in stage design, that the effects enhance qualities of place rather than overwhelm them.

Silver has selected pieces from his sculpture collection to ornament the grounds (figs. 184, 185, 192).[51] Reproductions of three sprites and several planters from Wright's Midway Gardens (Chicago, 1913–14, long since demolished), and reproductions of two cubic planters from the Storer house, sustain a Wrightian image without the usual rigidity of a museum, a limiting quality that Silver quite properly understands as foreign to the larger ideas Wright sought to express. And Silver continues to expand his collections. Thus when he discovered the chafing dishes used by Nina Lunn Stevens to ornament her lavish buffets, he acquired them to further enhance the layers of history embedded in the complex. And a classic station wagon (fig. 125), painted mint green as one of Stevens's own cars had been, led his daughter to ask if it were her father's.

Unseen in conventional views are other elements that further animate Auldbrass. For the first time ever, the plantation is staffed in the manner Wright knew would be necessary to sustain the elegant ease of so grand an estate. In addition to the manager are maids, gardeners, and other assistants; some help care for the friendly and apparently blissful group of dogs, cats, and birds that roam the estate. Also carefully tended are cattle that Silver raises. He favors Longhorns rather than the Brahmins raised by Stevens, finding their appearance more to his liking, but quarters them in some of the original pastures, all richly fenced with red pipe. Thus the plantation in part remains a working one.

For Silver and his many guests, Auldbrass provides extraordinary respite. Yet it has meant a major investment

OPPOSITE
FIG. 196

DOCK OFF RIVER HOUSE

Auldbrass; Eric Lloyd Wright. The "Karyn Anne" (pictured), acquired by Joel Silver in 1999 and named for his wife, is a twenty-two foot fantail launch that was built in 1913 to ply the waters of the Great Lakes.
Alan Weintraub/Arcaid, 2001

RIGHT
FIG. 197

RIVER HOUSE

Auldbrass; Eric Lloyd Wright. Anthony Peres, 2010

on Silver's part. By 1994, with work not even half done, he estimated that he had spent several million dollars on its completion.[52] Like Wright and Stevens before him, the project has become an unending quest, something ongoing. "Auldbrass will never be finished in my lifetime," he stated. "I'll build there until they bury me."[53] Also, like Stevens, he justifies his demanding professional involvements as a way of earning the vast sums necessary for Auldbrass: "Architecture is an expensive hobby. I've chosen the genre of commercial movies, because I need hits to pay for the restoration of these houses [Auldbrass and the Storer house]. Wright would have wanted it that way."[54] For Silver, living within a Wright-designed environment quite clearly offers a unique experience. "Everything about it— the spaces, materials, the grammar of the design, the plan of the house I live in—are all set in motion within an overall order. A day doesn't go by that I don't see something new, a new perspective."[55] He laments those who misunderstand Wright's approach. "Clients fight with Wright houses, but if you follow the grammar of the house, it works. Wright's way is better—not just the building, but everything."[56]

Silver's observations, as he is well aware, can only partly express the powerful image that Auldbrass now conveys. It can be argued that no bits of ruinous authenticity were better sacrificed to achieve aesthetic consistency, for the most essential part of Wright's vision—the living, changing continuity of architecture supportive of human life—has been regained. And within the ambit of surviving memory, perhaps the longest span of time within which such ambitious restoration can be rationalized, it has been recreated in a way that people want to remember. Stevens's daughter, upon seeing a newly restored portion for the first time, believed it to be exactly as her father had left it.[57] That nothing is ever really the same matters less, perhaps, than the impression of sameness, than the sense of history regained. In large part it accords with theories advanced by Caesare Brandi, who argues convincingly for artistic cohesion in buildings being restored, and supports the inclusion of new materials when no lost craft or radical change is involved.[58]

With the near completion of Auldbrass, a greater degree of Wright's original vision can be grasped. The low, horizontal emphasis of the angled and spreading roofs barely interrupt the skyline, seeming to stabilize and give shape to the low terrain. At the base of the walls, the angled supports lift the building slightly so it seems almost to hover over this terrain, amplifying an effect of screen-like lightness. Within, spaces seem to

open in every direction, without conventional closure. Surely no stronger sense of unity between building and place has ever been achieved, nor any place so enriched by architecture. Through Wright's interpretation the buildings not only complement the character of the site, they seem almost to create it, linking to those larger issues of order that he pursued. As all great art, Auldbrass offers much for further contemplation, and can inspire individual explanations of deeper meanings that enlarge its presence.

Through his efforts, Silver has done far more than provide momentary pleasures, for in pursuing the quest begun by Leigh Stevens and sustained by Stevens's daughter, he has realized a major design by Frank Lloyd Wright. The unity Wright sought to make tangible, that indivisible bond joining humanity with a changeable, even cosmic nature, can now be experienced.

EPILOGUE

In his introduction to the first edition of this book, published more than seven years ago, Joel Silver wrote, "Auldbrass continues to evolve. It continues to find new uses for itself while providing me new creative challenges. I am only a custodian of this testament to Frank Lloyd Wright's genius" (page 26). That has indeed been the case. With the addition of another child, Silver's family, too, has continued to change (fig. 203). So, too, has the appreciation of the historic locale of Auldbrass deepened, with nearby ruins of another time a reminder of the location's rich history. Highly evocative of this history are the ruins of Old Sheldon Church (fig. 204), known when completed in 1757 as Prince William Parish Church. In 1779, it was burned during the American Revolution; rebuilt in 1826, it was burned again during the Civil War, leaving only the columns and walls that remain today.[1]

Auldbrass itself continues to change in many ways, most dramatically with the incorporation of new elements. Three guest cottages have been added, located in conformance with Wright's early perspective (see fig. 23) identifying sites for three additional cabins that were never built (shown extending above the farm buildings at the top). As an understated indicator of their presence, a new fountain has been added at the end of the tack room (fig. 205), placed near the beginning of an almost hidden path that leads from the Wright-designed portions of the plantation to the new enclave of guest cottages beyond (figs. 206, 207). Its design, based on what Wright had designed to provide water for poultry, echoes the original use of the building as a chicken coop.

For these cottages, the architect Tom Crews adapted Wright's final design for a housekeeper's cottage (see fig. 115). This provided a more comfortable prototype than the staff cabins that Wright had originally suggested, for each has two bedrooms and a far more gracious living area than those one-room structures. By slightly altering the dimensions, Crews was able to insert a second bath, but otherwise adhered closely to Wright's plan and complicated profiles (fig. 208). As in the construction of the original buildings at Auldbrass, this proved to be no easy feat, and complications brought about by complex intersections required the same on-site resolution of details.[2]

Placed within an area of dense planting, the new guest cottages are not visible from the older portions of Auldbrass, but are positioned in a manner that generates beguiling glimpses from one to the other (fig. 209). They are identified by names reflecting predominant colors of interior furnishings: Bluebird (figs. 210, 211, 212, 213, 214), Teal (figs. 215, 216), and Rose (figs. 217, 218, 219). The names themselves are derived from those Wright had chosen, as part of the Taliesin Line, to identify custom paint colors to be manufactured by the Martin-Senour Company.[3] Screened porches expanding each cottage create lantern-like enclosures as well as protected areas for sitting outdoors. Inside, angles generated by the plan are amplified by details of the fireplaces, skylights, and glass doors. The original staff cabins, which had been adapted for guests during the initial restoration of Auldbrass, now swerve again for staff (see plot plan, fig. 156).

With its new guest rooms adding to others already present, Auldbrass can easily accommodate more than 30 guests in great comfort. But dealing with numbers of this sort led to a new addition: a grand piazza adjacent to the canal and its marina (figs. 220, 221), which can seat 60. Again this element is placed beyond the historic core of Auldbrass so it is not visible from those original structures, but instead generates a new identity. Again Crews has adapted a Wrightian vocabulary, this time to create a grand terrace for large-scale dining and entertainment.

Auldbrass itself continues to mature as all living structures do. Thus plantings have continued to grow, adding to the lushness of its setting (figs. 222, 223, 224). This is especially true along the stream paralleling the farm buildings, at last achieving an image that Wright must have imagined (fig. 225), and elsewhere Spanish Moss seems to have increased as well, reinforcing Wright's abstraction of that element in his detailing (figs. 226, 227). Newly photographed details record the cook shed's adaptation for guests (fig. 228) and the machine shed's completion with the dramatically angled trusses that Wright specified (fig. 229). Wright's own Lincoln Continentals, carefully restored under Silver's supervision, now take their place on the estate (fig. 230). Other images complete a picture of luxurious repose that now permeates the expansive setting (figs. 231, 232).

So, Auldbrass does indeed continue to evolve, as Silver had predicted. It has escaped the curse endured by many historic structures of being frozen in time without a sense of life; instead it continues to be adapted for new and vital uses, yet always with changes sensitive to Wright's original concept. Now more than ever it provides that sympathetic structure for the experience of place that Wright always so fervently sought.

—DAVID G. DE LONG
July 2010

FIG. 207
PATH TO NEW GUEST COTTAGES
Auldbrass. Anthony Peres, 2010

OPPOSITE TOP
FIG. 205
TACK ROOM
Auldbrass, with new fountain in foreground.
Anthony Peres, 2010

OPPOSITE BOTTOM
FIG. 206
COURTYARD
between barn and stable (at left) and tack room (at right) with path leading to new guest cottages at far rear. Anthony Peres, 2010

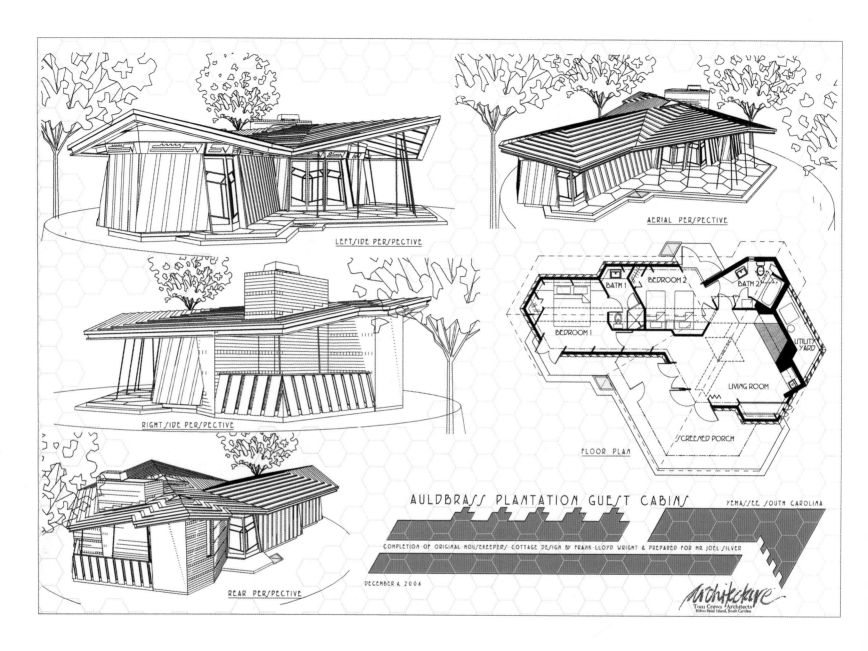

LEFTSIDE PERSPECTIVE

AERIAL PERSPECTIVE

RIGHTSIDE PERSPECTIVE

FLOOR PLAN

BEDROOM 1

BATH 1

BEDROOM 2

BATH 2

UTILITY YARD

LIVING ROOM

SCREENED PORCH

REAR PERSPECTIVE

AULDBRASS PLANTATION GUEST CABINS   YEMASSEE SOUTH CAROLINA

COMPLETION OF ORIGINAL HOUSEKEEPERS COTTAGE DESIGN BY FRANK LLOYD WRIGHT & PREPARED FOR MR JOEL SILVER

DECEMBER 4, 2004

Architecture
Tom Crews Architects
Hilton Head Island, South Carolina

FIG. 208
**PLAN AND PERSPECTIVES OF NEW
GUEST COTTAGES**

Auldbrass. Tom Crews, Architect

OPPOSITE
FIG. 209
**VIEW TO TEAL COTTAGE FROM
BLUEBIRD COTTAGE**

Auldbrass. Anthony Peres, 2010

FAR LEFT
FIG. 212
BLUEBIRD COTTAGE
Living room. Anthony Peres, 2010

ABOVE
FIG. 213
BLUEBIRD COTTAGE
Bedroom. Anthony Peres, 2010

LEFT
FIG. 214
BLUEBIRD COTTAGE
Bathroom for bedroom. Anthony Peres, 2010

LEFT

FIG. 215

TEAL COTTAGE
View from terrace to bedroom (left) and
porch Anthony Peres, 2010

ABOVE

FIG. 216

TEAL COTTAGE
Living room looking toward porch. Anthony
Peres, 2010

LEFT
FIG. 217
ROSE COTTAGE
Porch from outside. Anthony Peres, 2010

RIGHT
FIG. 218
ROSE COTTAGE
Porch. Anthony Peres, 2010

BELOW
FIG. 219
ROSE COTTAGE
Living room. Anthony Peres, 2010

ABOVE
FIG. 220
PIAZZA WITH MARINA AT LEFT
Anthony Peres, 2010

OPPOSITE
FIG. 221
PIAZZA SHOWING FIREPLACE DETAIL
Anthony Peres, 2010

LEFT

FIG. 222

**GARDEN ADJACENT
TO LIVING ROOM**
Auldbrass. Anthony Peres, 2010

BELOW

FIG. 223

**TERRACE ADJACENT TO LIVING
ROOM AND BEDROOMS**
Auldbrass. Anthony Peres, 2010

OPPOSITE

FIG. 224

**TERRACE DETAIL ADJACENT
TO LARGE BEDROOM**
Auldbrass. Anthony Peres, 2010

NOTES

INTRODUCTION

1. For an account of Fallingwater, Edgar Kaufmann, jr., *Fallingwater: A Frank Lloyd Wright Country House* (New York: Abbeville Press, 1986).
2. Together they prepared several publications, including Frank Lloyd Wright, *An American Architecture*, edited by Edgar Kaufmann [jr.] (New York: Horizon Press, 1955) and Frank Lloyd Wright, *Drawings for a Living Architecture* (New York: published for the Bear Run Foundation and the Edgar J. Kaufmann Charitable Foundation by Horizon Press, 1959).
3. Letter, Frank Lloyd Wright to Henry-Russell Hitchcock, November 23, 1940 (Frank Lloyd Wright papers, Avery Architectural Library, Columbia University in the City of New York), as cited in my review of *In the Nature of Materials*, published in *Architecture Plus* 1 (May, 1973), 13–15. I studied with both Kaufmann and Hitchcock while a graduate student at Columbia University.

A WRIGHT ANGLE

1. Futagawa, Yukio. *Houses of Frank Lloyd Wright*, GA Houses, Tokyo, 1975.

CHAPTER 1
LEIGH STEVENS AND
THE BEGINNINGS OF AULDBRASS

1. For Kaufmann, Edgar Kaufmann, jr., *Fallingwater: A Frank Lloyd Wright Country House* (New York: Abbeville Press, 1986); for Johnson, Jonathan Lipman, *Frank Lloyd Wright and the Johnson Wax Buildings* (New York: Rizzoli, 1986); for Price, Frank Lloyd Wright, *The Story of the Tower: The Tree That Escaped the Crowded Forest* (New York: Horizon Press, 1956).
2. For biographical information, I am indebted to Jessica Stevens Loring, Stevens's daughter, who has graciously allowed access to her archive of family memorabilia. Included in her records are correspondence, newspaper clippings, and other items cited below.
3. Letter, J. Charles Ireland and Leigh B. Smith to Master Charles Leigh Stevens, July 15, 1895, Jessica Stevens Loring papers.
4. C. Leigh Stevens, "The First Stevens' Seminar, October 21, 1952," 14-page typed manuscript of talk delivered at Harvard University, Jessica Stevens Loring papers; 4.
5. According to Jessica Loring Stevens, interview, May 22, 1993, and letter, Jessica Loring Stevens to David De Long, August 5, 1998.
6. Stevens, "First Seminar," 6.
7. According to Stevens's obituary in the *Muskegon Chronicle*, October 8, 1962, his sister, Mrs. Helen G. Edwards, was living in Sag Harbor, N.Y.
8. Stevens, "First Seminar," 5.
9. *Muskegon Chronicle*, October 8, 1962, and resumé of C. Leigh Stevens, Jessica Stevens Loring papers.
10. Letter, Dexter S. Kimball, Dean of the College of Engineering Cornell University, to C.L. Stevens, November 2, 1923. This committee action was also reported in a second letter, Herman Diederichs, Director of the Sibley School of Mechanical Engineering, to C. L. Stevens, November 2, 1923. Jessica Stevens Loring papers.
11. Stevens, "First Seminar," 7.
12. I am grateful to Jessica Stevens Loring for this family information. Her brother, Clifton Delmar Stevens, died on March 28, 1993. He left one daughter, Susan Leigh Stevens, born on February 2, 1946. Jessica Ann Stevens married Stanton Dunster Loring on January 14, 1942; their daughter, Jessica Loring, was born on December 20, 1943, and their grandson, Michael Loring Mayne, was born on September 17, 1973.
13. Biographical information on Bedaux is drawn from Jim Christy, *The Price of Power; A Biography of Charles Eugene Bedaux* (Toronto and Garden City, N.Y.: Doubleday, 1984). I am grateful to Joel Silver for leading me to information on Bedaux.
14. Ibid., especially 66, 150.
15. Stevens, "First Seminar," 6–12. Also, Christy, 59.
16. Nina Lunn Stevens, *Genius Slams the Door*, unpublished manuscript, partly unpaginated, in the Frank Lloyd Wright Archive, The Frank Lloyd Wright Foundation, Taliesin West (hereafter FLWA). I am grateful to Joel Silver for sharing his copy of this manuscript. Nina Lunn was Stevens's third wife, as will be discussed.
17. W. Arnold Hosmer, J. Leslie Rollins, and Raymond W. Miller, "C. Leigh Stevens," *Harvard University Gazette*, March 16, 1963; reprinted, *Harvard Business School Bulletin*, April–May 1963; reprinted as, "C. Leigh Stevens; Memorial Minute Adopted by the Faculty of Business Administration, Harvard University", undated.
18. Stevens, "First Seminar," 12.
19. Copy, letter of recommendation, Donald K. David (name of addressee not indicated), January 8, 1953, Jessica Stevens Loring papers.
20. Memorandum, "Seminar in Production by C. Leigh Stevens," enclosed with letter from Richard Chapin, Harvard University Graduate School of Business Administration, to C. Leigh Stevens, December 7, 1950, Jessica Stevens Loring papers. In the letter, Chapin states, "the enclosed is a rough attempt at putting your two memoranda together."
21. C. Leigh Stevens, resumé (undated); Jessica Loring Stevens papers.
22. Stevens, "First Seminar," 12.
23. C. Leigh Stevens, undated resumé; Jessica Stevens Loring papers.
24. Memorandum, C. Leigh Stevens to Dean Teele, February 27, 1952; these principles were repeated in a memorandum from William D. Swan, Jr., to Associate Dean Stanley F. Teele reporting on C. L. Stevens Seminars, July 1, 1953; both documents, Jessica Stevens Loring papers.
25. Stevens, "First Seminar," 7-8.
26. Letter, Arthur B. Chapin, President of the American Trust Company, to C. Leigh Stevens, October 29, 1927. Attached to the letter is a newspaper clipping naming Stevens as president of the Reed-Prentice Co.; "Chapin Heads American Trust Co." (no source listed), date inscribed, October 26, 1927; Jessica Stevens Loring papers.
27. As noted in Leland M. Roth, *American Architecture: A History* (Boulder, Colorado: Westview Press, 2000), 354. The firm of William Graves Perry, Thomas Mott Shaw, and Andrew H. Hepburn are also featured as being "retained to have charge of the architectural development of the plan" in *The Restoration of Colonial Williamsburg in Virginia* (reprinted from *The Architectural Record* 78, December 1935; New York: F.W. Dodge, 1935), 357. The working drawings for Stevens's house by Perry, Shaw & Hepburn, 177 State Street, Boston, are dated December 28, 1925, with revisions dated December 30, 1925. They are entitled, "Cottage for C. L. Stevens, Esq., at Westwood, Massachusetts." These drawings are among Jessica Stevens Loring papers. In 1993, the descendant firm practiced under the name Perry, Dean & Rogers.
28. Letter, Jessica Stevens Loring to David De Long, May 24, 1993.
29. Interview, Jessica Stevens Loring, May 22, 1993. The house was published in a local Boston newspaper, where it was described as "the gardener's house on the estate of C. Leigh Stevens." The clipping, inscribed 1928 but with no source noted, is in the possession of Jessica Stevens Loring.
30. Letter, Jessica Stevens Loring to David De Long, August 5, 1998.
31. Interview, Jessica Stevens Loring and Stanton D. Loring, May 23, 1993.
32. Contract between Savannah River Lumber Corporation and C. Leigh Stevens, December 20, 1938; Jessica Stevens Loring papers.
33. Miles O. Hayes and Walter J. Sexton, *Modern Clastic Depositional Environments: South Carolina* (Washington, D.C.: American Geophysical Union, 1989), 59.
34. Soler and Mills, "Surficial Geology and Geomorphol-

ogy," in Horton, Jr., J. Wright and Victor A. Zullo, editors, *The Geology of the Carolinas* (Carolina Geological Survey Fiftieth Anniversary Volume; Knoxville: University of Tennessee Press, 1991), 299.

35. Horton, Jr., J. Wright and Victor A. Zullo, "An Introduction to the geology of the Carolinas," in Horton, Jr., J. Wright and Victor A. Zullo, editors, *The Geology of the Carolinas*, 6.

36. Hayes and Sexton, *Modern Clastic Depositional Environments*, 1.

37. Jessica Stevens Loring, *Auldbrass: The Plantation Complex Designed by Frank Lloyd Wright; A Documented History of Its South Carolina Lands* (Greenville, South Carolina: Southern Historical Press, 1992).

38. Ibid., 1.

39. Richard S. Dunn, "The English Sugar Islands and the Founding of South Carolina," *The South Carolina Historical Magazine* 72, April 1971, 81–93.

40. Loring, *Auldbrass*, 7–8.

41. Interview with Joel Silver, May 25, 2002.

42. Loring, *Auldbrass*, 13.

43. Nicholas Olsberg, *Desolate Places; The South Carolina Chivalry at the Time of the Civil War*, undated manuscript, the South Carolina Historical Society, Charleston; 61–73; based on his earlier dissertation written under the name, Robert Nicholas Olsberg, *A Government of Class and Race: William Trescot and the South Carolina Chivalry, 1860–65* (Ph.D. Dissertation: University of South Carolina, 1972).

44. Aspects of this are discussed in Robert Withers Allston, *Memoir of the Introduction and Planting of Rice in South-Carolina* (Charleston: Miller & Browne, 1843), especially 1, 7, 18.

45. Olsberg, *Desolate Places*, especially 82, 139–140, 166.

46. William Elliott, *Carolina Sports By Land & Water* (Charleston: Burges and James, 1846; facsimile edition, New York: Arno Press, 1967), 109. For a biographical note on Elliott, Beverly Scafidel, "The Author-Planter William Elliott (1788–1863)," *The Proceedings of the South Carolina Historical Association* 1981, 114–119.

47. Richard J. Amundson, "Trescot, Sanford, and Sea Island Cotton," *The South Carolina Historical Magazine* 68 (1967), 31–36.

48. William Henry Trescot, *Oration Delivered Before the Alumni of the College of Charleston, June 25, 1889* (Charleston: Walker, Evans and Cogswell, 1889), 5, 11. The description of Trescot is found in David Moltke-Hansen, "A Beaufort Planter's Rhetorical World; The Contexts and Contents of William Henry Trescot's Orations," *The Proceedings of the South Carolina Historical Association* 1981, 120–132.

49. Elliott, *Carolina Sports By Land & Water*, especially 83, 92, 107.

50. Loring, *Auldbrass*, 31.

51. Katharine N. McNulty with Jessica Stevens Loring, Stanton Loring, and Cindy Cole, National Register Form for Old Brass (historic name) or Auldbrass (current name), October 17, 1975, 14 pages. A copy of this form is filed with the Auldbrass folder, South Carolina Historical Society, Charleston.

52. Letter, Jessica Stevens Loring to David De Long, August 5, 1998; also, interview, May 22, 1993. Leigh Stevens related a similar story to Nina Lunn Stevens, as reported by her in *Genius Slams the Door*, 8.

53. Among sources for this story is R. Angus Murdoch, Executive Director, Historic Charleston Foundation, in a Letter to the Editor filed with the Auldbrass folder, South Carolina Historical Society, Charleston. A similar story was related to me by Simon Jinks at Auldbrass in the spring of 1987; Jessica Stevens Loring believes Jinks story was the source of Murdoch's letter.

54. Letter, Jessica Stevens Loring to David De Long, August 5, 1998.

55. Loring, *Auldbrass*, especially 124–131. For the general history of the area during this time, 121–123.

56. Interview, Nicholas Olsberg, June, 1992. I am grateful to Olsberg for sharing his knowledge of the area.

57. "Mepkin Plantation, Moncks Corner, S.C., Winter Home for Mr. and Mrs. Henry R. Luce; Edward D. Stone, Architect," *Architectural Forum* 66 (June, 1937), 515–522. Also, Edward Durell Stone, *The Evolution of an Architect* (New York: Horizon Press, 1962), 33–51; and W. A. Swanberg, *Luce and His Empire* (New York: Charles Scribners, 1972), 133. The pattern of northerners enjoying winter retreat in the area is also discussed in Gunther Stamm, "Frank Lloyd Wright's Auld Brass Plantation: Preliminary Remarks," text of a paper presented at the College Art Association Convention, 1974; typed manuscript in the possession of Jessica and Stanton Loring. Also, Gunther Stamm, "Modern Architecture and the Plantation Nostalgia of the 1930s: Stone's 'Mepkin' and Wright's 'Auldbrass Plantation'" (abstract of a talk presented at the Annual Meeting), *Journal of the Society of Architectural Historians* 34 (December, 1975), 318. For additional information on Luce, W. A. Swanberg, *Luce and His Empire* (New York: Scribners, 1972).

58. Interviews with Jessica Stevens Loring, July 17, 1992, and May 22, 1993. For mention of Big Survey, John H. Davis, *The Guggenheims; An American Epic* (New York: William Morrow and Co., 1978), 198.

59. Matt Lee and Ted Lee, "Rice Fields Cultivate Old Ways; In South Carolina Low Country, wildlife and down-home cooking along the roads and creeks of the ACE Basin," *The New York Times* (February 25, 2001, Travel Section), 10, 29. The ACE Basin refers to the area drained by the Ashepoo, Combahee, and Edisto Rivers.

CHAPTER 2
FRANK LLOYD WRIGHT
AND THE DESIGN OF AULDBRASS

1. For the most moving account of his life, Frank Lloyd Wright, *An Autobiography* (London, New York, and Toronto: Longmans, Green and Company, 1932; second revised and expanded edition, New York: Duell, Sloan and Pearce, 1943). Other, more recent biographies include Brendan Gill, *Many Masks: A Life of Frank Lloyd Wright* (New York: G.P. Putnam's, 1987) and Meryle Secrest, *Frank Lloyd Wright* (New York: Alfred A. Knopf, 1992).

2. For an account of these years, David G. De Long, "Frank Lloyd Wright: Designs for an American Landscape," in *Frank Lloyd Wright: Designs for an American Landscape*, edited by David G. De Long (New York: Harry N. Abrams in association with the Canadian Centre for Architecture, the Library of Congress, and the Frank Lloyd Wright Foundation, 1996), 15–133.

3. Upon her divorce from Vlademar Hinzenberg Lazovich on April 8, 1925, Olgivanna had assumed her mother's maiden name of Milanoff according to Robert Sweeney, "Frank Lloyd Wright Chronology, 1922–1932," in *Frank Lloyd Wright: Designs for an American Landscape, 1922–1932*, 192.

4. Interview, Joel Silver, May 25, 2002. Silver sees several parallels between Auldbrass and Wright's own homes in Wisconsin and Arizona; for example, the hexagonal pool designed for Auldbrass resembles a similar, though much smaller, reflecting pool at Taliesin West.

5. Letter, C. L. Stevens to Frank Lloyd Wright, December 18, 1938; FLWA.

6. Interviews, Jessica Stevens Loring, July 17, 1992, and May 22, 1993.

7. Bibliographers have noted nearly 30 articles in 1938 alone; Robert L. Sweeney, *Frank Lloyd Wright; An Annotated Bibliography* (Los Angeles: Hennessey & Ingalls, 1978), 62–68.

8. "Usonian Architect," *Time* 31 (January 17, 1938), 29–32 and cover.

9. Frank Lloyd Wright, "Frank Lloyd Wright," *Architectural Forum* 68 (January, 1938), special issue.

10. *Architectural Forum* (January, 1938); Taliesin, 2–23; Wingspread, 56–63.

11. As quoted in Nina Lunn Stevens, *Genius Slams the Door*, 10, 58.

12. Ibid., 9.

13. Ibid., 10, 23.

14. Ibid., 59. Jessica Stevens Loring also stated that her father wanted Auldbrass to be a fully working plantation from the beginning, as well as a private retreat; interview, July 17, 1992.

15. Letter, C. L. Stevens to Frank Lloyd Wright, April 3, 1939; FLWA.

16. Ibid.

17. As recalled by Nina Lunn Stevens, *Genius Slams the Door*: Alice Ravenel Huger Smith, *A Carolina Rice Plantation of the Fifties* (New York: W. Morrow, 1936), illustrated with watercolors of the lowlands, and Frances Marion Hutson and John R. Todd, *Prince Williams Parish and Plantations* (Richmond: Garrett & Massie, 1935). Both include traditional images of the sort typical in such books of the period, as noted below. According to Bruce Brooks Pfeiffer, Director of the Frank Lloyd Wright Archives, the copies in Wright's library are well-thumbed. Of course they could have arrived in such condition.

18. As recounted in Kaufmann, *Fallingwater*, 39–41.

19. Letter, C. L. Stevens to Frank Lloyd Wright, August 14, 1939, FLWA.

20. Undated notes filed with Auldbrass correspondence, FLWA.

21. Nina Lunn Stevens, *Genius Slams the Door*, 73.

22. As recounted throughout *The Natural House* (New York: Horizon Press, 1954).

23. Nina Lunn Stevens, *Genius Slams the Door*, 59.

24. Telegram, C. L. Stevens to Frank Lloyd Wright, October 26, 1939; FLWA. Wright's handwritten reply was drafted on the bottom of the telegram.

25. Telegram, C. L. Stevens to Frank Lloyd Wright, November 10, 1939, FLWA.

26. Letter, Eugene Masselink to C. L. Stevens, November 18,

1939; FLWA.

27. Letter, Frank Lloyd Wright to C. L. Stevens, November 20, 1939; telegram, Frank Lloyd Wright to C. L. Stevens, November 28, 1939; telegram, Frank Lloyd Wright to C. L. Stevens, December 15, 1939; telegram, C. L. Stevens to Frank Lloyd Wright, December 18, 1939; FLWA.

28. In the lower right, Wright has annotated the drawing, "Stevens 'Auldbrass' 1940." This date is not necessarily accurate. As Henry-Russell Hitchcock frequently remarked (interviews, 1971–74), Wright sometimes dated drawings well after they were completed, especially when working with Hitchcock to produce the first major monograph of his work, *In the Nature of Materials*.

29. Drawings 4015.003, 4015.004, FLWA.

30. Telegram, Frank Lloyd Wright to C. L. Stevens, January 18, 1940, FLWA.

31. Beginning around 1951, Stevens's third wife, Nina Lunn Stevens, began referring to the cook shed as a gate house; Jessica Stevens Loring believes this was "apparently to dignify the entrance to the main house," letter to David De Long, August 5, 1998.

32. Telegram, Frank Lloyd Wright to C. L. Stevens, March 15, 1940; FLWA.

33. Letter, C. L. Stevens to Frank Lloyd Wright, April 21, 1940, FLWA.

34. Letter, C. L. Stevens to Frank Lloyd Wright, May 25, 1940; FLWA.

35. Ibid.

36. Interview, Jessica Stevens Loring, May 22, 1993.

37. I am grateful for Jessica Stevens Loring and Stanton Loring for reviewing the legal documents with me and for summarizing the key issues; interview, May 22, 1993.

38. Letter, Frank Lloyd Wright to C. L. Stevens, April 24, 1940; FLWA.

39. Letter, Joseph N. Welch to C. L. Stevens, January 4, 1946; Jessica Stevens Loring papers.

CHAPTER 3
GEOMETRIC INVENTION
IN THE SHAPING OF AULDBRASS

1. For a longer summary, and one on which I base my own, Edgar Kaufmann, jr., "Frank Lloyd Wright: Plasticity, Continuity, and Ornament," *Journal of the Society of Architectural Historians* 37 (March, 1978), reprinted, Edgar Kaufmann, jr., *9 Commentaries on Frank Lloyd Wright* (New York, Cambridge, Massachusetts, and London: The Architectural History Foundation and The MIT Press, 1989), 119–127.

2. De Long, "Designs for An American Landscape," 15–16.

3. For example, Edgar Kaufmann, jr., "'Form' became 'Feeling', A New View of Froebel and Wright," *Journal of the Society of Architectural Historians* 39 (May, 1980), 145–49; reprinted, Kaufmann, *9 Commentaries*, 1–6.

4. Frank Lloyd Wright, *An Autobiography* (1932), reprinted in Bruce Brooks Pfeiffer, *Frank Lloyd Wright: Collected Writings*, 5 vols. (New York: Rizzoli, 1992–95), vol. 2, 234.

5. Ibid., 111.

6. Eugene-Emmanuel Viollet-Le-Duc, *Discourses on Architecture*, translated by Henry Van Brunt (Boston: James R. Osgood, 1875), First Discourse, 14. He later returns to this theme; for example, Tenth Discourse, 491–497, 510.

7. Ibid., Sixth Discourse, 182. The term "nature of materials"—to be much used also by Wright—occurs in several places, for example, Eighth Discourse, 332, and Tenth Discourse, 490, 510.

8. Ibid., Tenth Discourse, 509.

9. Ibid., Ninth Discourse, 414.

10. Ibid., 450.

11. Among early editions, Eugene-Emmanuel Viollet-Le-Duc, *Dictionnaire Raisonné de L'Architecture* 10 volumes (Paris: A. Morel, 1869); for the diagram in question, vol. 8, 485. I am grateful to Narciso Menocal for bringing this theory to my attention and for directing me to its source. For information on its obscure translation and Wright's relation to it, Donald Hoffman, "Frank Lloyd Wright and Viollet-le-Duc," *Journal of the Society of Architectural Historians* 28 (October 1969), 173–183.

12. Among descriptions, William L. MacDonald, *The Architecture of the Roman Empire, Vol. I, An Introductory Study* (New Haven and London: Yale University Press, 1965), especially 31–41.

13. Frank Lloyd Wright, *Architectural Forum* 88 (January, 1938), 64.

14. Frank Lloyd Wright, "In the Cause of Architecture III: The Meaning of Materials—Stone", *Architectural Record* 63 (April, 1928), 350–356; reprinted, Pfeiffer, *Collected Writings* I, 275.

15. Anthony Alofsin convincingly demonstrates how Wright's fascination with rotated forms can be traced to his early stays in Europe in 1909–11; Anthony Alofsin, *Frank Lloyd Wright; the Lost Years, 1910–1922* (Chicago and London, University of Chicago Press, 1993), 39, 260. Also of interest is the doctoral dissertation by Richard Joncas, *'Pure Form:' The Origins and Development of Frank Lloyd Wright's Non-Rectangular Geometry* (Stanford University: Dissertation submitted to the Department of Art, 1991).

16. Frank Lloyd Wright, *Architectural Forum* 88 (January, 1938), 68.

17. "Frank Lloyd Wright Designs a Honeycomb House," *Architectural Record* 84 (July, 1938), 59–74.

18. Curtis Besinger, *Working with Mr. Wright; What It was Like* (New York: Cambridge University Press, 1995), 118. I worked with Professor Besinger on editing the early versions of this manuscript for the Architectural History Foundation, and we discussed Auldbrass on several occasions.

19. The term, its various uses, and various sources are discussed by Neil Levine in *The Architecture of Frank Lloyd Wright* (Princeton University Press, 1996), especially 169. For other texts relating to angled geometries, Levine, 478, note 94.

20. For a brief history of the Inglenook and Wright's exploitation of that element, Edgar Kaufmann, jr. "Precedent and Progress in the Work of Frank Lloyd Wright," *Journal of the Society of Architectural Historians* 39 (May, 1980), 145–49; reprinted in *9 Commentaries on Frank Lloyd Wright*, 67–74.

21. Frank Lloyd Wright, "Frank Lloyd Wright," *Architectural Forum* 88 (January, 1948), special issue, 95.

22. Frank Lloyd Wright, *Taliesin Drawings; Recent Architecture of Frank Lloyd Wright Selected from His Drawings* with comments by Edgar Kaufmann, jr. (New York: Wittenborn, Schultz, 1952), 62.

23. Curtis Besinger, *Working with Mr. Wright; What It Was Like*, 90–91.

24. Frank Lloyd Wright notes [1940], filed with Stevens correspondence, FLWA.

25. For example, letter, C. L. Stevens to Frank Lloyd Wright, April 21, 1940; FLWA.

26. Katharine N. McNulty with Jessica Stevens Loring, Stanton D. Loring, and Cindy Cole, National Register Nomination of Auldbrass Plantation, October 17, 1975. A copy of this form is on file at the South Carolina Historical Society, Charleston.

27. Interview, Jessica Stevens Loring, July 17, 1992.

28. Especially John R. Todd and Francis M. Hutson, *Prince Williams Parish and Plantations* (Richmond, Virginia: Garrett & Massie, 1935), 120, 122, 128, 148, 243. Highly evocative of the area's landscape are watercolors illustrating Alice Ravenel Huger Smith, *A Carolina Rice Plantation of the Fifties* (New York: W. Morrow, 1936). Bruce Brooks Pfeiffer, who has organized the Frank Lloyd Wright Archives at Taliesin West, observed that Wright's copy of Smith's book especially shows signs of much use; interview, Joel Silver, May 25, 2002.

29. Frank Lloyd Wright, *Architectural Forum* (January, 1948), 95.

30. Letter, Jessica Stevens Loring to David De Long, July 29, 1999.

31. Frank Lloyd Wright, "A Philosophy of Fine Art" (1900); reprinted, Pfeiffer, *Collected Writings*, I, 43.

32. Frank Lloyd Wright, *Architectural Forum* (January 1948), 95.

CHAPTER 4
BUILDING AULDBRASS: THE FIRST CAMPAIGN

1. Signed agreement between J. J. McDevitt Company and C. L. Stevens, September 21, 1940, filed with court records, McDevitt & Street Company versus C. Leigh Stevens et al., State of South Carolina, County of Beaufort, Roll No. 4065, R.M.C. Office for Beaufort County. I am grateful to Jessica Stevens Loring and Stanton D. Loring for discovering these documents and for sending me copies.

2. Working drawings, FLWA. For the involvement of Jack Howe, I am grateful to Jonathan Lipman, Prairie Architects, Inc., Fairfield, Iowa, for interviewing Howe regarding the design and construction of Auldbrass, and for transmitting the information to me (letter, June 23, 1993).

3. Letter, C. L. Stevens to Frank Lloyd Wright, August 19, 1940; FLWA.

4. Telegrams, Frank Lloyd Wright to C. L. Stevens, August 24, 1940, August 27, 1940; letter with statement of expenses for September 23–24 and September 25 to October 22, Peter Berndtson to C. L. Stevens, November 1, 1940; FLWA.

5. Proposal for Building and Utilities—Auldbrass Plantation, filed with court records, McDevitt versus Stevens.

6. Ibid.

7. Ibid.

8. Agreement between J. J. McDevitt Company and C. L. Stevens, filed with court records, McDevitt versus Stevens.

9. Eight typed pages of questions [from Stevens] with answers signed F.L.L.W., 1940; filed with Stevens correspondence, FLWA.

10. Ibid.

11. Billings filed with court records, McDevitt versus Stevens, indicate suppliers, including: canvas, Savannah Ship Chandlery & Supply Co.; cypress, R.L. McLeod & Son; roofing, The Sisalkraft Co. (copper covered Sisalkraft); bronze shoes, Queen City Foundry; plumbing fixtures, Crane; wax, Sinfassal; glass, Pittsburgh Plate; flitch plates and bolts, Southern Engineering Company.

12. Eight-page memo, 1940; FLWA.

13. Typed text for telegram annotated in Wright's hand, Frank Lloyd Wright to C. L. Stevens, November 27, 1940, FLWA.

14. Telegram, Wesley Peters to Frank Lloyd Wright, November 28, 1940; FLWA.

15. Telegram, Frank Lloyd Wright to C. L. Stevens, December 7, 1940; FLWA.

16. Telegram, Wesley Peters to Frank Lloyd Wright, December 10, 1940; letter, C. L. Stevens to Frank Lloyd Wright, February 1, 1941; FLWA.

17. Letter, T. F. Haddock for McDevitt Co. to William Wesley Peters, December 3, 1940; Letter, Wesley Peters to Peter Berndtson, December 14, 1940; Letter, Eugene Masselink to C. L. Stevens, December 17, 1940; FLWA.

18. Letters, Wesley Peters to Peter Berndtson, December 14, 1940; Eugene Masselink to C. L. Stevens, December 17, 1940; FLWA.

19. Letter, T. F. Haddock to Peter Berndtson and Eugene Masselink, December 12, 1940; FLWA.

20. Letters, Eugene Masselink to McDevitt Co., February 14, 1941; T. F. Haddock to Frank Lloyd Wright, February 19, 1941; drawing, "Framing Diagrams, Passageways,", 4015.025, March 3, 1941; FLWA.

21. Telegram, Frank Lloyd Wright to C. L. Stevens, February 22, 1941; FLWA. Drawing showing sections for farm buildings, 4028.005, August 7, 1940, revised February 24, 1941.

22. Nina Lunn Stevens, *Genius Slams the Door*, 101.

23. Telegram, C. L. Stevens to Frank Lloyd Wright, April 29, 1941; FLWA.

24. Letter, T. F. Haddock to Wesley Peters, May 23, 1941; FLWA.

25. Caretaker's Cottage at Auldbrass, Sheet 3, Elevations, August 7, 1940; 4025.006, FLWA; pencil alterations to drawing undated.

26. Letter, Jessica Stevens Loring to David De Long, August 5, 1998.

27. Aeroshade's products are described in *Sweet's Catalogue File* (New York: F. W. Dodge, 1939), vol. 16, 93. Their lack of materials is documented by a letter, The Aeroshade Company, Aerolux Window Shades, Waukesha, Wisc., to Wes Peters, June 5, 1941; FLWA.

28. Drawing, "Furniture Details," 4015.024, March 3, 1941; revised May 26, 1941.

29. Letter, C. L. Stevens to Frank Lloyd Wright, June 17, 1941; FLWA.

30. Plot plan 40.014A, undated.

31. "Revised Layout. . .", 4015.016, FLWA.

32. "Revised Layout. . .", 4015.017, FLWA.

33. Telegram, C. L. Stevens to Frank Lloyd Wright, July 24,

34. Telegram, Frank Lloyd Wright to C. L. Stevens, July 26, 1941; FLWA.

35. Letter of transmittal, Eugene Masselink to C. L. Stevens, August 12, 1941; FLWA.

36. Telegram, C. L. Stevens to Frank Lloyd Wright, August 6, 1941; FLWA.

37. Letter of transmittal, Eugene Masselink to C. L. Stevens, August 7, 1941; FLWA.

38. Interview, Jessica Stevens Loring, July 17, 1992.

39. Letter, Wesley Peters to Theodore Lyman, May 22, 1942; FLWA. The visit would have occurred between May 9 and May 22.

40. Nina Lunn Stevens, *Genius Slams the Door*, 56.

41. Letter, C. L. Stevens to McDevitt & Street Co., August 21, 1941, filed with court records, McDevitt versus Stevens.

42. Telegram, C. L. Stevens to Frank Lloyd Wright, August 6, 1941; telegram, Frank Lloyd Wright to T. F. Haddock, August 7, 1941, FLWA.

43. Letter, T. F. Haddock to Wesley Peters, September 26, 1941; letter, Wesley Peters to T. F. Haddock, October 8, 1941, FLWA.

44. Letter, C. L. Stevens to Frank Lloyd Wright, September 4, 1941; FLWA.

45. For example, letter accepting "most of your changes," Frank Lloyd Wright to C. L. Stevens, September 15, 1941; FLWA.

46. Letter, T. F. Haddock to Wesley Peters, September 26, 1941; FLWA.

47. Letter, T. F. Haddock to Wesley Peters, October 27, 1941; FLWA.

48. For example, letters, McDevitt Construction Company to Wesley Peters, October 29, 1941; C. L. Stevens to T. F. Haddock, November 4, 1941; Eugene Masselink to the Crane Company, November 8, 1941; Crane Company to Frank Lloyd Wright, November 17, 1941; Wesley Peters to Hoffman Hardware, November 29, 1941; Wesley Peters to Wolfe, Kubly and Hirsig Co. [hardware], November 29, 1941; FLWA.

49. Letters, Wesley Peters to Lyman, Inc., Montclair, New Jersey, November 3, 1941; Wesley Peters to Gillen Woodworking Corporation, Milwaukee, November 3, 1941; Hoffman to T. F. Haddock, December 4, 1941; FLWA.

50. Letter, C. L. Stevens to Frank Lloyd Wright, December 5, 1941; FLWA.

51. Letter, McDevitt Construction Co. to Frank Lloyd Wright, October 27, 1941; FLWA.

52. I am grateful to Joel Silver for sharing his copies of 21 photographs which he recalled obtaining from the South Carolina Historical Society in Charleston. According to Mike Coker of the Society, they have no such pictures (telephone interview, September 10, 2002). Calls to the *Charleston News and Courier* (now the *Post and Courier*) and to the *Charlotte Observer* also turned up nothing.

53. *Charleston News and Courier* (December 21, 1941), Section II, 14, as cited in Kenneth Severens, *Southern Architecture; 350 Years of Distinctive American Buildings* (New York: E. P. Dutton, 1981), 167–170. I have been unable to verify this date, or the exact title; according to newspaper employees with whom I spoke in 1992, copies no longer existed, and I have been unable to locate an archive of back issues.

54. Interview, Jessica Stevens Loring, July 17, 1992.

55. Sam A. Cothran, "The 'Crazy Plantation' Near Yemassee,

S.C. Has Native Folk A-Talking—and Swooning! Right Angles and Verticles [sic] are Ruled Out," *Charlotte Sunday Observer* (January 4, 1942), Section Four, 1, 2. I am grateful to Joel Silver for providing me with a copy of this story. It is also mentioned in Severens, *Southern Architecture*, 167–70.

56. Letter, C. L. Stevens to Frank Lloyd Wright, January 5, 1942; FLWA.

57. Ibid.

58. For a discussion of the St. Gall plan, Kenneth John Conant, *Carolingian and Romanesque Architecture, 800 to 1200*, revised edition (Baltimore: Penguin Books, 1974), 55–59.

59. Letter, C. L. Stevens to Frank Lloyd Wright, January 5, 1942; FLWA.

60. Court records, McDevitt versus Stevens.

61. Letter, C. L. Stevens to McDevitt & Street, December 31, 1942, filed with court records, McDevitt versus Stevens.

62. Drawing, "Miscellaneous Details," 4015.041; May 20, 1942, signed "O.K. FLLW, June 7/42;" FLWA.

63. Letter, George S. Affleck to C. L. Stevens, December 19, 1942; FLWA. In later years, the Lorings used Cabot's clear creosote on the exterior; letter, Jessica Stevens Loring to David De Long, August 5, 1998.

64. Interview, Jessica Stevens Loring, May 22, 1993.

65. Letter, Wesley Peters to John T. Lyman, February 20, 1942; FLWA.

66. Letter, John T. Lyman to Wesley Peters, May 8, 1942; FLWA.

67. Letter, Wesley Peters to Theodore Lyman, May 9, 1942; FLWA.

68. Letters, Martin H. Feinman for Modernage Furniture Corporation, Miami Beach, Florida, to Frank Lloyd Wright, March 5, 1942; Frank Lloyd Wright to C. L. Stevens, March 17, 1942; FLWA. Among advertisements for Modernage, *House and Garden* 70 (October 1936), 14. Among advertising booklets, *House of the Modern Age* (Modernage Furniture Corporation, Park Avenue at 39th Street, New York, ca. 1936; the Avery Art and Architectural Library at Columbia University has one copy).

69. Letter, Interior Decorating Division, Marshall Field & Company, to Frank Lloyd Wright, January 7, 1942; FLWA.

70. Letters, Robert W. Funk, for Marshall Field & Company, to C. L. Stevens, December 19, 1942; December 23, 1942; FLWA.

71. Letter, Robert W. Funk for Marshall Field & Company to Frank Lloyd Wright, December 28, 1942; FLWA.

72. Letter, Robert W. Funk for Marshall Field & Co. to C. L. Stevens, December 29, 1942; FLWA.

73. Telegram urging Stevens to open account at Marshall Field, Frank Lloyd Wright to C. L. Stevens, January 9, 1943; letter, Robert W. Funk for Marshall Field & Company to Frank Lloyd Wright, January 11, 1943; letter, Eugene Masselink to Robert W. Funk, January 13, 1943; FLWA. The estimate for the carpet was evidently sent to Stevens at some later date, as later references will suggest, but has not been found.

74. Notes by Bruce Brooks Pfeiffer in Bruce Brooks Pfeiffer, Editor, Frank Lloyd Wright, *Collected Writings*, 4 vols. (New York: Rizzoli in association with the Frank Lloyd Wright Foundation, 1992–95), vol. 4, 109.

75. Frank Lloyd Wright, "Concerning Marcus Weston's Fel-

lowship at Taliesin," Pfeiffer, Vol. 4, 111. [109–111]

76. Letter with enclosed petition, Frank Lloyd Wright to C. L. Stevens, February 6, 1943; FLWA; also, Jessica Stevens Loring papers.

77. Petition, together with the letter to Stevens requesting his signature on a slightly shortened version, February 6, 1943; Jessica Stevens Loring papers.

78. Interview, Jessica Stevens Loring, May 22, 1993. Stevens's description of himself as "a dollar-a-year man" is also repeated in correspondence; letter, Theodore Lyman to Theodore Baird, undated [1943 or 1944], Theodore Baird correspondence file, FLWA. I am grateful to Bruce Brooks Pfeiffer for bringing the Baird correspondence to my attention.

79. "C. Leigh Stevens; Memorial Minute Adopted by the Faculty of Business Administration," Harvard University; reprinted from the Harvard University Gazette, March 16, 1963; also, letter, Richard Chapin to C. L. Stevens, December 7, 1950; Jessica Stevens Loring papers.

80. Letter, Frank Lloyd Wright to C. L. Stevens, March 9, 1945; Jessica Stevens Loring papers.

81. Letter, Theodore Lyman to Theodore Baird, September 27, [1942], Theodore Baird correspondence file, FLWA.

82. Letters, Theodore Lyman to Theodore Baird, February 4, [1943?] and August 27 [1943?], FLWA.

83. Letter, Theodore Lyman to Theodore Baird, undated [1944?], FLWA.

84. Letter, Theodore Lyman to Theodore Baird, January 22, 1945, FLWA.

85. McDevitt versus Stevens, court records.

86. McDevitt versus Stevens, court records.

87. McDevitt versus Stevens, December 13, 1943, filed with court records.

88. Report of the Special Referee, April 27, 1944, filed with court records, McDevitt versus Stevens.

89. Court records, McDevitt versus Stevens.

90. A later article reported hearsay evidence that the house was completed in 1942 at a cost of around $200,000; "Auld Brass House Near Yemassee Built By Wright," Charleston News and Courier, April 10, 1959. The library of the newspaper was only begun in the late 1940s and does not contain earlier copies.

CHAPTER 5
BUILDING AULDBRASS:
THE LATER CAMPAIGNS

1. Interview, Curtis Besinger, April, 1992; also, letter summarizing interview with John (Jack) Howe, Jonathan Lipman to David De Long, June 2, 1993.

2. Nina Lunn Stevens, Genius Slams the Door, unpublished manuscript, FLWA, copy courtesy of Joel Silver; 11.

3. Information on Stevens's family comes primarily from his daughter, Jessica Stevens Loring.

4. W. Arnold Hosmer, "C. Leigh Stevens," Harvard Business School Bulletin (April–May 1963), 23–24.

5. Nina Lunn Stevens, 72.

6. Nina Lunn Stevens, 91. Correspondence in the Frank Lloyd Wright Archive supports this contention.

7. Letter, C. L. Stevens to Frank Lloyd Wright, April 1, 1946; FLWA.

8. A retainer of $500 is noted in the letter, C. L. Stevens to Frank Lloyd Wright, April 27, 1946. Letters arranging the meeting include Frank Lloyd Wright to C. L. Stevens,

April 17, 1946, with directions on how to reach Taliesin West; and C. L. Stevens to Frank Lloyd Wright confirming their meeting, April 19, 1946; FLWA.

9. Letter, C. L. Stevens to Frank Lloyd Wright, May 4, 1946; FLWA.

10. Letter, Frank Lloyd Wright to C. L. Stevens, May 13, 1946; FLWA.

11. Letter, C. L. Stevens to Frank Lloyd Wright, October 25, 1946; FLWA.

12. Interview, Jessica Stevens Loring, July 17, 1992.

13. Lounge Chair, 4015.089, revised December 1, 1946; drawing archive at Auldbrass. Revised Furniture for C. L. Stevens, 4015.046, March 1, 1946; FLWA.

14. New working drawings for the guest house are dated "Revised November 1, 1946," and signed November 3, 1946; plans, 4024.009, 4024.010; the altered elevation, 4024.011; FLWA.

15. Drawings dated December 1, 1946, include 4015.043 and 4015.044.

16. Layout of Auldbrass, March 1, 1947, 4015.018; FLWA.

17. Telegram, Frank Lloyd Wright to C. L. Stevens, January 15, 1948; FLWA.

18. "Frank Lloyd Wright," special issue, Architectural Forum 88 (January, 1948), 65–156; Auldbrass, 95–96. Other publications followed, although Auldbrass was not as widely published as other of Wright's designs. Among sources not listed elsewhere in this volume, Werner Moser, Frank Lloyd Wright: Sixty Years of Living Architecture (Zurich, 1952), 88–89; Frank Lloyd Wright, An American Architecture, edited by Edgar Kaufmann [jr.] (New York: 1955), 232; Frank Lloyd Wright, Drawings for a Living Architecture [edited by Edgar Kaufmann, jr.], (New York: 1959), 94–97; Edgar Kaufmann and Ben Raeburn, Frank Lloyd Wright: Writings and Buildings (New York, 1960), 335; William Allin Storrer, The Architecture of Frank Lloyd Wright; A Complete Catalogue (Cambridge, Massachusetts and London, 1974), 261–264. Auldbrass had been included, but not illustrated or discussed in any detail, in Henry-Russell Hitchcock, In the Nature of Materials (New York, 1942), 130.

19. Interview, Jessica Stevens Loring, July 17, 1992.

20. Letter of appointment, Secretary of Harvard College for the President and Fellows, October 4, 1948; Jessica Stevens Loring papers.

21. Hosmer, "C. Leigh Stevens;" also, Memorandum, William D. Swan, Jr., to Associate Dean Stanley F. Teele, reporting on C. L. Stevens's seminars, July 1, 1953; Jessica Stevens Loring papers.

22. Letter, Jessica Stevens Loring to David De Long, August 5, 1998.

23. Nina Lunn Stevens, 5, 25.

24. Nina Lunn Stevens, 27.

25. Nina Katherine Lunn, Physical Attraction and Your Hormones; A Modern Guide to Beauty, Vitality, and Health (Garden City, N.Y.: Doubleday & Co., 1950). An author's note claims that the book "culminates 5 years of reading and digesting the medical literature in the hormone field. . .", and Chapter 2 is titled, "What Is the Secret of Sexual Attraction?".

26. Nina Lunn Stevens, 1–5. Information of Senator White comes from Jo Anne McCormick Quantannens, Senators of the United States; A Historical Bibliography (Washington, DC: GPO, 1995), 298; it lists no bibliographic

entries. Nina's relationship to White was confirmed by her granddaughter, Nina Black; telephone interview, November 23, 2002. She referred to Auldbrass as her "grandparents' house."

27. The Senator Was Indiscreet starred William Powell and was directed by George S. Kaufman with a screenplay by Charles Mac Arthur; it is available on videotape.

28. Nina Lunn Stevens, 40.

29. Nina Lunn Stevens, 80, 85, 89. The supervising farmer, Mr. Bright Youmans, is quoted in the text.

30. Nina Lunn Stevens, 115, 118.

31. Nina Lunn Stevens, 98.

32. Nina Lunn Stevens, 164.

33. Nina Lunn Stevens, 165. Stevens's daughter remembers that Nina had been primarily responsible for getting another designer for the furniture; interview, May 22, 1993.

34. According to Olga Guelft, "Edward J. Wormley: A Portrait," [Contract] Interiors, November 1956, 92–105.

35. Ibid.

36. Nina Lunn Stevens, 165–171. A print of Wormley's drawing, dated August 14, 1951, is in the archive at Auldbrass (4015.125).

37. Drawings include Additions and Alterations to Main House, 4015.047 and House as Revised, 4015.048 (both dated September 17, 1951); FLWA.

38. Telegram, Frank Lloyd Wright to C. L. Stevens, October 16, 1951; FLWA.

39. Nina Lunn Stevens, 172.

40. Nina Lunn Stevens, 174.

41. Nina Lunn Stevens, 195–196.

42. Letter, C. L. Stevens to Frank Lloyd Wright, January 28, 1953; FLWA, Getty microfiche. The tone of the letter suggests that it had happened several months earlier; Nina Lunn Stevens (207) wrote that it occurred in March; by elimination, presumably March, 1952.

43. Nina Lunn Stevens, 207–210.

44. Nina Lunn Stevens, 211–213.

45. The date is confirmed by a letter, C. L. Stevens to Frank Lloyd Wright, January 28, 1953; FLWA.

46. As reported by Nina Lunn Stevens, 113.

47. Interview, Bruce Brooks Pfeiffer, September 3, 1997. Pfeiffer was one of the three apprentices; the others were John Rattenbury and John Amaramitides.

48. Nina Lunn Stevens, 236. Her accounts of problems leading to this letter, 220, 223, 233–35. Her ship from Europe, the Constitution, docked in New York on February 7, 1953; Stevens's letter was dated February 5, 1953.

49. Letter, C. L. Stevens to Frank Lloyd Wright, January 28, 1953; FLWA.

50. Letter, Frank Lloyd Wright to C. L. Stevens, February 13, 1953; FLWA.

51. Letter, C. L. Stevens to Frank Lloyd Wright, March 11, 1953; FLWA.

52. Letter, Frank Lloyd Wright to C. L. Stevens, March 16, 1953; FLWA.

53. Among many publications of his work, "Thomas Church: His Gardens," Architectural Forum 83 (August 1945), 111–118.

54. Nina Lunn Stevens, 177.

55. The landscape plan by Thomas Church is dated April 3, 1952; Auldbrass archive. There is no record of the Auldbrass commission in the Thomas Church Collection in the Environmental Design Archives at he University of Cali-

fornia, Berkeley; e-mail, Carrie McDade, Assistant Curator, to David De Long, October 28, 2002. According to Mark Treib, Professor of Architecture at Berkeley who has recently completed monograph on Church, Church did not keep records on all his commissions; e-mail, Treib to De Long, October 24, 2002. Treib also reports that correspondence in the Church Collection confirms at least one visit by Church to Auldbrass.

56. Aerogram, C. L. Stevens to Frank Lloyd Wright, April 8, 1953; FLWA.

57. Letter, Frank Lloyd Wright to C. L. Stevens, April 18, 1953; FLWA.

58. Telegram, C. L. Stevens to Frank Lloyd Wright, April 20, 1953; FLWA.

59. A copy of the drawing with Wright's comments is preserved in the Auldbrass archive and numbered 4015.117. Stevens thanks Wright for his comments in a letter, C. L. Stevens to Frank Lloyd Wright, June 15, 1953; FLWA.

60. Nina Lunn Stevens, 175.

61. The formally drafted plan, titled, "New Dining Room," and indicated as revised, is dated August 1953; FLWA.

62. Letter, Jessica Stevens Loring to David De Long, July 29, 1999.

63. "Indian Device is Brainchild of S.C. Native," *Charleston News and Courier* (July 26, 1958), clipping filed with folder on Auldbrass, South Carolina Historical Society, Charleston. According to the article, Stevens toured India in 1954, at the invitation of the Ministry of Community Development. In a typed news release dated July 25, 1958, the date of the tour is given as 1953 and the Ministry as that of Commerce and Industry. The news release is credited to the Ford Foundation, but the lack of any official letterhead suggests otherwise; Jessica Stevens Loring papers.

64. "High Voltage Bullocks Are Brainchild of Yemassee Man," *Charleston News and Courier* (December 21, 1958), clipping filed with information on Auldbrass, South Carolina Historical Society, Charleston.

65. Nina Lunn Stevens, from unpaginated portion of manuscript; also, letter, Jessica Stevens Loring to David De Long, August 5, 1998.

66. Letters, Jessica Stevens Loring to David De Long, July 29, 1999; August 5, 1998. Also, interview, Simon Jinks, May 24, 1987. Jinks performed occasional odd jobs for Stevens in the early 1960s.

67. M. G. Kains, *Five Acres and Independence; a Practical Guide to the Selection and Management of the Small Farm*, revised edition (New York: Greenberg, 1935; 12th printing, 1942), 5. My copy of this book, which had been Stevens's, was given to me by Jessica Stevens Loring. Other books in his library included L. H. Bailey, *The Cultivated Conifers in North America* (New York: MacMillan, 1933); L. H. Bailey, *The Standard Cyclopedia of Horticulture*, 3 volumes (New York: MacMillan, 1937 (volumes 1 and 2) and 1961 (volume 3); P. P. Pirone, *Maintenance of Shade and Ornamental Trees* (New York: Oxford University Press, 1941); George A. Martin, *Fences, Gates and Bridges* (Springfield, Massachusetts: Orange Judd Company, 1909); R. P. Clarkson, *Practical Talks of farm Engineering* (New York: Doubleday, Page & Company, 1915); and *How To Do Things*, a compendium from *The Farm Journal* (Philadelphia: Wilmer Atkinson Company, 1919). I am grateful to Jessica Stevens Loring for this information.

68. Nina Lunn Stevens, unpaginated section of manuscript.

69. Interview, Simon Jinks, May 24, 1987.

70. Nina Lunn Stevens, 270–274.

71. Nina Lunn Stevens, 253, 288.

72. Nina Lunn Stevens, 261, 268.

73. Nina Lunn Stevens, unpaginated section and 307, 311,321. According to an entry in Jessica Stevens Loring's diary of April 17, 1964, it was constructed by Dawson Engineering Company of Charleston. She recalls that it had been built during Nina's stay. Letter, Jessica Stevens Loring to David De Long, December 8, 1998.

74. Although the cottage was later demolished by Joel Silver, I saw it on my first visit to Auldbrass in 1987.

75. Nina Lunn Stevens, 255 and unpaginated portion of manuscript.

76. Nina Lunn Stevens, 316.

77. Letter, Nina Lunn Stevens to Mrs. Frank Lloyd Wright, March 25, 1957; FLWA. In this letter, Nina refers to their meeting with Wright in New York the previous week.

78. Letter, Eugene Masselink to Nina Lunn Stevens, May 15, 1957; FLWA. According to Masselink, Wright was then "en route Baghdad via Paris, Rome, and Cairo."

79. According to a written memorandum from Jessica Stevens Loring, they were divorced on June 18, 1957.

80. Nina Lunn Stevens, 321.

81. Interview, Jessica Stevens Loring, May 22, 1993.

82. Obituaries, October 8, 1962: *The Boston Herald*, *The Boston Globe*, *The Boston Traveler*, *The New York Times*, *New York Herald Tribune*, and *The Muskegon Chronicle*. According to records maintained by Jessica Stevens Loring, Stevens's first wife, Jessica Agnes Thompson Stevens, died on September 11, 1969; the date of death of Stevens's second wife, Ann, is not known; Nina Lunn Stevens died on January 20, 1992; Barbara Berger Honeyman Stevens died on April 3, 1999.

83. Letter, C. L. Stevens to Douglas Ensiminger, of the Ford Foundation, February 24, 1962; FLWA.

84. W. Arnold Hosmer, "C. Leigh Stevens," *Harvard Business School Bulletin*, April–May, 1963; also, brochure explaining this program, "Self Aid to Education"; Jessica Stevens Loring papers.

85. Nina Lunn Stevens, 165.

CHAPTER 6
JESSICA STEVENS LORING
AND THE SURVIVAL OF AULDBRASS

1. Letters, Jessica Stevens Loring to David De Long, December 8, 1998, and September 20, 1999. Mrs. Loring adds that the manager of the Savannah River Lumber Corporation was assisted in his duties as executor by a trust company in Savannah, as stipulated in Stevens's will.

2. Letter, Jessica Stevens Loring to David De Long, December 8, 1998.

3. Interview, Jessica Stevens Loring, July 17, 1992.

4. The area figures were calculated for Joel Silver at the time he purchased the property; interview, Joel Silver, October 24, 1998.

5. Interview, Jessica Stevens Loring, May 22, 1993.

6. Letter, Jessica Stevens Loring to David De Long, December 8, 1998.

7. Ibid.

8. Wiliam Allin Storrer, *The Architecture of Frank Lloyd Wright; A Complete Catalog* (Cambridge, Mass., and London: the MIT Press, 1974).

9. Letter, Jessica Stevens Loring to David De Long, December 8, 1998.

10. "Auldbrass Plantation On National Register," *The Press and Standard*, December 2, 1976 (clipping in the possession of Jessica Stevens Loring). A copy of the informational document accompanying the listing is filed with the Auldbrass material at the South Carolina Historical Society in Charleston.

11. Letters, Jessica Stevens Loring to David De Long, September 20, 1999, and May 23, 1994. The sale of the property was handled by William P. Baldwin and Associates, of Summerville, S.C.; brochures advertising the property are in the possession of Jessica Stevens Loring. Among other notices, the sale was advertised in the *Frank Lloyd Wright Newsletter* 1 (July–August, 1978), 8.

12. "Frank Lloyd Wright's Auldbrass," sales brochure for William P. Baldwin and Associates, in the possession of Jessica Stevens Loring.

13. Mrs. Loring showed the stored furniture to R. Craig Miller, then Associate Curator in the American Wing, in February 1981. He selected pieces for the Metropolitan's collection. Mrs. Loring later retrieved the prints from Avery Library, wanting to loan them to Joel Silver when he was beginning the restoration of Auldbrass. Silver had the prints organized and catalogued, placing copies in a private archive he established at Auldbrass. He returned the original prints to Mrs. Loring together with one of the duplicate sets. He also gave sets to Eric Lloyd Wright, his architect of choice for the restoration. Letter, Jessica Stevens Loring to David De Long, September 20, 1999. Also, interview, R. Craig Miller, 1999.

14. They were included in the sale of American arts and crafts auctioned at Sotheby's on November 19, 1981, according to the auction catalogue in the possession of Jessica Stevens Loring. The listing in the catalogue includes chairs, hassocks, bookcases, low hexagonal tables, a portion of the clerestory frame, and other miscellaneous items, lots 263–293.

15. Information on the transfer of the property is drawn from Rank P. Jarrell, "Auldbrass Art the Wright Stuff," *Charleston News and Courier*, November 3, 1989; and Letter to the Editor from R. Angus Murdoch, Executive Director, Historic Charleston Foundation, undated. The clipping and letter are filed with the Auldbrass papers, South Carolina Historical Society, Charleston.

16. Interviews, Joel Silver, October 24–25, 1998, and May 25–26, 2002.

17. I met Donna Butler in the fall of 1998; the Butler Appraisal Company was then located at 839 Meriweather Drive, Savannah, GA, 31406. Also, notes, Donna Butler to David DeLong, September 19, 2002.

18. Interview, Joel Silver, May 25, 2002; letter, Donna R. Butler, Preservation Consultant for Chapman Appraisal Company, Inc., Real Estate Appraisers & Consultants, Savannah, to Jessica Stevens Loring, February 20, 1987. in the possession of Jessica Stevens Loring.

19. Although they began to hold meetings in the mid 1980s, The Frank Lloyd Wright Building Conservancy was not officially formed until June 1989, according to "Frank Lloyd Wright in the Valley of the Sun," announcement of

the Frank Lloyd Wright Building Conservancy Annual Conference, Scottsdale, Ariz., November 10–14, 1999. As of 2002, the Conservancy is located at 5132 South Woodlawn Avenue, Chicago, Ill., 60615.

20. Interview, Thomas Schmidt, November 23, 1998.
21. Silver's restoration of the Storer house is described in Pilar Viladas, "Wright in Hollywood," *House and Garden* 162 (February 1990), 78–87, and Victoria Newhouse, "Joel Silver; The Producer's Frank Lloyd Wright House in Los Angeles," *Architectural Digest* 55 (April 1998), 278–287, 315.
22. Interview, Thomas Schmidt, September 20, 2002.
23. Interviews, Thomas Schmidt, November 23, 1998, and Joel Silver, November 15, 2002.
24. Letter, Jessica Stevens Loring to David De Long, December 6, 1998.

CHAPTER 7
JOEL SILVER AND
THE COMPLETION OF AULDBRASS

1. Interview, Joel Silver, May 26, 2002.
2. Interviews, Joel Silver, July 17, 1992; October 24–25, 1998; and May 26, 2002. Also, interview, Thomas Schmidt, November 23, 1998. I am grateful to Mr. Schmidt and Mr. Silver for sharing these details of sale with me.
3. Silver initially purchased the property in partnership with two friends, but assumed full ownership within a year. The agreement of sale was with the Beaufort County OpenLand Trust, which deeded the property to Silver and his associates. Interview, Joel Silver, May 26, 2002.
4. In addition to interviews with Joel Silver, which I have had since 1987, biographical information is drawn from an interview conducted by Suzanne Stephens, *The AHF Review* (The Architectural History Foundation, New York, Spring–Summer, 1993), 2, 4; and Mark Singer, "The Joel Silver Show," The *New Yorker* (March 21, 1994), 122–129.
5. Silver relates that his sister later led him to books on Wright that had once belonged to Douglas Haskell and Helen Lacey, and these he acquired; interview, Joel Silver, May 26, 2002.
6. Singer, 124.
7. Ibid.
8. As quoted in Singer, 124–125.
9. Singer, 125, 129.
10. Herbert Muschamp, "If the Cityscape is Only a Dream," *New York Times*, May 2, 1999.
11. John Ruskin, *The Seven Lamps of Architecture* (1849; reprinted, New York: Farrar, Straus and Cudahy, 1961); "The Lamp of Memory," 186.
12. This painstaking effort is recorded in Zarine Weil, editor, *Building A Legacy; The Restoration of Frank Lloyd Wright's Oak Park Home and Studio* (San Francisco: Pomegranate Press in association with the Frank Lloyd Wright Preservation Trust, 2001), especially 34. Also, Elaine Harrington, *Frank Lloyd Wright Home and Studio, Oak Park* (Stuttgart: Edition Axel Menges, 1996).
13. Interview, H. Allan Brooks, April, 1998. Brooks served as a member of the committee making recommendations for the restoration, and he strongly opposed this course of action.

14. As exhibited at the Canadian Centre for Architecture, Montreal, May 26 to October 31, 1999, and illustrated in the accompanying catalogue: Nicholas Olsberg, George Ranalli [et al.], *Carlo Scarpa Architect; Intervening with History* (Montreal and New York: Canadian Centre for Architecture and the Monacelli Press, 1999).
15. Nicholas Olsberg, "Introduction," *Carlo Scarpa*, 13.
16. George Ranalli, "The Palazzo Abatellis. . . Extended," *Carlo Scarpa*, 48.
17. Eugene Emmanuel Viollet-le-Duc, "On Restoration," *Dictionaire raisonné de l'architecture française du XIe au XVIe siecle*, 10 vols., reprinted as "Defining the Nature of Restoration," M. F. Hearn, editor, *The Architectural Theory of Viollet-le-Duc: Readings and Commentary* (Cambridge, Mass.: The MIT Press, 1990), 269.
18. For an article examining the completion of unfinished works, Jenny Lyn Bader, "The Art of Finishing Unfinished Art," *The New York Times*, May 30, 1999.
19. Ruskin, "The Lamp of Memory," 186.
20. Suzanne Stephens, "Interview with Joel Silver," 4.
21. For illustrations of the work completed at a comparatively early stage, Brendan Gill, "Frank Lloyd Wright's Auldbrass; A Film Producer Restores the Architect's Forgotten Plantation Complex in South Carolina," *Architectural Digest* 50 (December 1993), 126–37, 180–81.
22. For recent illustrations of much of this work, Brendan Gill, "Frank Lloyd Wright's Auldbrass".
23. Frank Lloyd Wright, The London Lectures, 1939, as published in *The Future of Architecture* (New York: Horizon Press, 1953), 288, 290.
24. Interview, Joel Silver, May 26, 2002.
25. The beginning of work is noted in Eric Lloyd Wright, "Auldbrass; Restoration of a 20th Century Plantation," *Frank Lloyd Wright Quarterly* 2 (Autumn, 1991), 3–5. Construction on the main house is reported in Kathleen Campisano, "The Crazy house; Renovation under way on Wright-designed plantation," *Low Country Sunday*, August 14, 1988. Completion of construction on the main house is reported in "Auldbrass Plantation; Phase One Restoration Complete," *FLlW Update* 1 (September–October, 1989), 3.
26. As recorded in working drawings by Island Mechanical and dated 1989; Auldbrass.
27. Interview, Joel Silver, October 24–25, 1998.
28. The symposium, "Preserving Wright's Heritage," was billed as the third annual symposium sponsored by Domino's Pizza in collaboration with the University of Michigan.
29. Interview, Joel Silver, October 24–25, 1998.
30. Ibid.
31. Spellings of this product vary; I have transcribed this spelling from one of the cans at Auldbrass.
32. Interview, Joel Silver, October 24–25, 1998.
33. Ibid.
34. Silver recalls the New Jersey company's name as Soneborn and the product's name as Windsor Wax; interviews, October 24–25, 1998, and November 15, 2002.
35. Silver reports that the owner of this company has since died; interview, May 26, 2002.
36. The Bathroom Plan by Eric Lloyd Wright is numbered 4015.106 and dated April 26, 1989; Auldbrass.
37. Interview, Joel Silver, May 26, 2002.
38. As recorded in working drawings, "New Dining Room. . .

Restoration Architect Eric Lloyd Wright," 4015.104, November 3, 1988; Auldbrass archive.
39. Stevens had three modular tables and twelve matching side chairs built according to Wright's design for the main living room. These Mrs. Loring sold at auction; letter, Jessica Stevens Loring to David De Long, September 20, 1999. In addition to those pieces built for the new dining area, Silver rebuilt those for the main living room as well.
40. Wright's original "Lounge Chair" is recorded in drawings 4015.089 and 4015.090, dated December 1, 1946. Eric Lloyd Wright's realization of this chair, and his designs of other pieces, are recorded in drawings 4015.111–113; they include an "Adirondack Chair," December 12, 1989; and an "Outside Chair," February 15, 1990, and March 26, 1990; Auldbrass archive.
41. Letter, Jessica Stevens Loring to David De Long, August 5, 1998.
42. The new tube lights are manufactured by Lumaline; interview, Eric Lloyd Wright, June 2, 1993.
43. Interview, Scott McNair, October 25, 1998.
44. Drawings for the rebuilding of the staff cabins by Eric Lloyd Wright are numbered 4030.026 and dated March 28, 1990; Auldbrass archive.
45. Interview, Eric Lloyd Wright, June 2, 1993.
46. Working drawings for the pool are by Crystal Pools; numbers include 4097.001–006, dated 1988; Auldbrass archive.
47. The working drawings in Eric Lloyd Wright's office (which I examined in 1993) are dated 1992 and include drawings number 4024.023–26; copies are also located in the Auldbrass archive.
48. As detailed in Anne Whiston Spirn, "Frank Lloyd Wright; Architect of Landscape," in *Frank Lloyd Wright; Designs for an American Landscape, 1922–1932*, edited by David G. De Long (New York: Harry N. Abrams in association with the Canadian Centre for Architecture, the Library of Congress, and the Frank Lloyd Wright Foundation, 1996), 135–169.
49. Interviews, Eric Lloyd Wright, June 2, 1993; Joel Silver, October 24–25, 1998.
50. The history of these cars is recounted in Dave Cole, "The Lincoln Continentals," *Frank Lloyd Wright Quarterly* 8 (Spring, 1997), 14–17. The Cabriolet is pictured before Auldbrass in Paul Goldberger, "Machines for Living: The Architectonic Allure of the Automobile," *Architectural Digest* 53 (October 1996), 82, 86, 90.
51. Silver's collection is discussed in Rebecca Mead, "Arts and Crafts; A Richard Serra fan ponders the artist's demographics," *The New Yorker* (September 28, 1998), 32.
52. Singer, 126.
53. Ibid.
54. Suzanne Stephens, "Interview with Joel Silver," 4.
55. Suzanne Stephens, "Interview with Joel Silver," 2.
56. Interview, Joel Silver, October 24–25, 1998.
57. I was with Mrs. Loring on this visit to Auldbrass in June, 1992, arranged so that I might record her impression.
58. As presented in Cesare Brandi, "Theory of Restoration" (1963), in *Historical and Philosophical Issues in the Conservation of Cultural Heritage*, Nicholas Stanley Price, M. Kirby Talley, Jr., and Alessandra Melucco Vaccaro, editors (Los Angeles: The Getty Conservation Institute, 1996), 230–235, 339–342, and 377–379.

EPILOGUE

1. Information comes in part from Alexia Chianis, "South Carolina: Old Sheldon Church Ruins" (June 1, 2006).
2. I am grateful to Tom Crews and Scott McNair, the manager at Auldbrass, for showing me through these new buildings and discussing their design and construction with me on my last visit to Auldbrass in November, 2009. Other details of changes at Auldbrass were provided by Margaret Martin, assistant manager; I am grateful to her not only for information she provided, but also for the her hospitality in making my visit comfortable as well.
3. As discussed in David A. Hanks, *The Decorative Designs of Frank Lloyd Wright* (New York: E.P. Dutton, 1979), 198.

INDEX

FOLLOWING PAGES
FIG. 232
VIEW ACROSS LAKE
Auldbrass. Anthony Peres, 2010